Goodbye Old Pick

"And Where is the Colliers Battlefeild (sic)"
asks Charles Lawton

A compelling true story of the life of
a coal miner facing daily the hazards
of the fiery pits of Staffordshire
in the nineteenth century.
by
Ann Goddard

A tribute to her great grandfather
Charles Lawton 1839 — 1921

Published by

J & A Goddard
1 Plains Lane, Blackbrook
Belper, DE56 2DD

First published in this format in UK 2005

References and Acknowledgements

Grateful acknowledgement is made for the extensive use that has been made of the contemporaneous reports published in the Staffordshire Weekly and Daily Sentinel, the Colliery Guardian, Keates & Ford's Review of 1866 and the Parliamentary Reports of 1867 to the Secretary of State for the Home Department (The Right Hon. S.H.Walpole MP) in highlighting the background of Charles Lawton's remarkable manuscript.

Other information was obtained with his blessing, from "A Journal of a Derbyshire Pitman 1835–1906", by Terry Judge and in private correspondence with Maurice Deakin, C Eng. F.I.Min.E. from his long experience as a mining engineer.

CONTENTS

PREFACE
BY THE RT HON PATRICK MCLOUGHLIN MP

I have known Ann Goddard for a number of years as a campaigner for the Derbyshire countryside.

In this book, Ann turns her attention to an aspect of her family history. It tells the story of her great grandfather, Charles Lawton between 1839 and 1921. Charles was a coal miner, rising to the position of colliery manager, but working also to improve the lot of his fellow miners.

Charles worked underground in the Staffordshire coalfields, as I did and my father and grandfather before me, which is why Ann kindly invited me to introduce her book.

As I write, we are all worried by the threat to our safety by international terrorism. I believe, however, that it is a good time to remember the hazards that our forefathers encountered every day. Every time they went down a pit – or to the many other dangerous industries – they risked their lives, and every day they did so increased the risk to their health.

Ann has done well to bring this alive through her great grandfather's work and writing, and to trace the remarkable history of one such worker.

Rt Hon Patrick McLoughlin MP, September 2005
Member of Parliament for West Derbyshire.

Charles Lawton

CHAPTER ONE

'COMETH THE HOUR, COMETH THE MAN'

SETTING THE SCENE

When this manuscript came into my hands in 1995 I read it, probably the first person to do so in almost one hundred years, with wonder and amazement. Wonder that such prose could flow from the pen of a man who had left school at the age of eight, and amazement that its worth had been unrecognised by so many for so long. It came to me on the death of my aunt, sister to my mother and granddaughter to Charles Lawton. I knew immediately that it must be published and, because it was in the form of an address to some gathering, I had no fears that I would be revealing matters that would better remain concealed. The copperplate script, though for the most part meticulous, was not easy to read, but the quality of the language with its overtones of Primitive Methodist 'ranting' was reward enough for any amount of effort expended. Add to this the liberal sprinkling of Staffordshire dialect interspersed with technical colliery terms and you will have some idea of my predicament. I am indebted to Terry Judge, a respected local Mining Historian and an author in his own right, for his help in unwinding some of the intricacies of the text. He enthused me, guided me towards sources of information and provided the background detail so essential for a true understanding of the Coal Mining Industry as experienced by Charles Lawton. Sadly Terry died suddenly and unexpectedly in June, 1996. I missed his 'drive' and experience and I wasted a lot of time before returning to the script.

To appreciate the story we must get to know the man and the social structure of his day. This was the time of the twitching lace curtain. The facade of respectability presented an impervious front to the world. The tragedies, trials and tantrums of the domestic hearth never saw the light of day. All tribulations were borne with a fierce pride, a self-respect and a stoicism few would find possible today. Not for them the weeping on the social worker's shoulder nor the baring of the soul on the counsellor's couch. They knew poverty, hardship and exploitation such as we can scarcely imagine, but there was no escape. They were in the grip of a system desperately in need of change, but who was to change it?

'Cometh the Hour, Cometh the Man'

Would it be perhaps the 'landed gentry'? No indeed! They were happy with their lot, living in luxury in the 'big house' comfortably distant from the working classes that earned them their wealth and tended their needs. As my great-grandfather writes in 'A Reminiscence of a Collier's Life'

> "I'm making the ladies and gentlemen warm
> Though I ain't got no latin or learning
> I get them their coals for winter and storm
> But they don't think of me while they're burning."

There was a certain air of 'noblesse oblige' and some were indeed great benefactors, but there were also many more that ruled with the iron rod showing little mercy to the workman who failed in his duty or forgot 'his place'. Shall we look then for our reformer in the middle ranks? Here we shall reap even less reward. For we find the man who has, by fair means or foul, managed to raise himself from the drudgery of the most menial tasks and now, using the little power he has, enforces his master's will with cruelty, greed and corruption. Scant chance of help from him then as he sees his escape route clearly before him.

So, it fell to the Charles Lawtons of the Coal Mining Industry to try to improve the lot of their fellow men. Their England consisted of a few major cities, several large towns and a multitude of villages and hamlets, based around centres of industry but widely scattered and strongly individual in culture and character. Communication was difficult; travel was slow, dangerous and expensive. Few moved far from their village. There was little awareness of the larger canvas and other obstacles lay in their path. They had brief formal education. Charles himself seems to be largely self-educated, gleaning his basic skills of literacy and numeracy from Sunday school. Only much later, shaken by his own harrowing experiences in the notoriously dangerous fiery pits of Staffordshire, was he motivated to attend evening classes where he refined his natural talents and gained the qualifications necessary to ensure his passport to promotion. He knew his voice would only be heard if he spoke with sincerity from a position of authority. Miners were poor and the calls upon what few resources they had were many. Sick pay and unemployment benefits were undreamt of and every scrap of medical care put pressure on the straitened family purse. Working hours were long, payment was by results and holidays a rare luxury enjoyed by but a few. There was little energy left to engage in battles with the establishment in the search for better conditions. So they laboured on, sustaining each other in a comradeship that has survived to this day although the industry has changed beyond recognition. Altered lifestyles and scientific advances have together reduced the need for deep mined coal and many a once thriving mining community has had its heart and spirit broken.

Charles Lawton entered this world on April 23, 1839 in the most inauspicious circumstances. We believe that he may have been the illegitimate son of a collier's daughter. He drew his first breath, and many a subsequent one in a collier's cottage in Butt Lane, Kidsgrove, Staffordshire. Throughout his reminiscences he speaks with great affection of his mother but there is nowhere mention of his father nor of any siblings. I think it is fairly safe to assume that, had there been others, they would have worked alongside him at the pit. He would surely, aged only ten have walked beside his father or his brothers to his first working day underground. He tells of playing in "my mother's garden" and of "My Dear mother's tears" when he returned from work. He ceased full time education, if indeed he ever attended on a regular basis, at the age of eight and ran errands above ground at the pit until, at the age of ten, he was able to start on his chosen career and take his first "stent" underground. One day he would fulfil his ambition to wear the collier's flannel jacket, cap and clogs but he endured much hardship before reaching his goal. His memoirs tell their own story.

At the age of nineteen he became a father for the first time. Matilda was born and his wife, Elizabeth was to bear him three more children at intervals of two years, namely Frank, Luther and Lilla. It must have come as a considerable shock to them to learn of the impending arrival of a fifth child some eight years later. This was my grandmother, Hannah, who was the apple of Charles' eye — his "Nancy" — who enjoyed a much more privileged childhood than her brothers and sisters, being born, as she was, when Charles was beginning to make his mark. By this time he had risen to the position of under manager and had many harrowing experiences behind him. I think he was a hard man, I know he was a very brave man and it is clear that he had gained the respect and esteem of many connected with the Coal Mining Industry. He was now directing his energies to bettering the working conditions of the coal miner. He determined to make the pit face a safer place to be, to bring all the women and children out of the workings, rescuing them from the abuse they suffered at the hands of crude and uneducated men. He saw the injustice of it all. He recognised the inhumanity of the demands made by the owners and above all he abhorred an industry that demanded of its work force that they toiled in Stygian gloom, that they spent most of their daylight hours entombed amidst choking dust with the constant threat of gas fed explosion. To reach their workplace they were obliged to crawl along the flooded roads for miles, a day's hard labour in itself and all unpaid. He had educated himself and, maybe because of his humble beginnings, he was determined to be heard.

What a wordsmith is here, when writing for the page or speaking to a listening throng. His phrase is crafted with the Latin scholar's skill, words chosen with a poet's ear and all as rhythmic as a lilting melody. You'll travel with the miner to his place of work, you'll hear his song, weep with the man who prays and share a mother's guilt. There is a story too, as D. H. Lawrence wrote, that will, perhaps, recall to mind the Eastwood miners walking to Goose Fair in Nottingham to "go in" for such larks the day they got their pay. Charles Lawton and his mates did not get their day off though he enjoys relating the story.

But 'ware the undertow! The undercurrent carries passion and emotion. Make no mistake. This man is angry, bitter and frustrated. His pen strokes score the sheet with letters bold and large, his words o'erflow the margins of the page paying scant regard to spelling and punctuation. His pent–up fury seeks release. The Coal Kings of the day would indeed have "*trembled in their shoes*" to hear the voice of Public Opinion so eloquently raised to champion the miners' cause. And, at the end, the Hymn of Praise to those who spend their lifetime in the dark to earn a crust and "*keep the roses in their little children's cheeks.*"

He wrote papers and gave lectures to many audiences including the Institute of Mining and Mechanical Engineers of which he was elected a founder member in December 1872 and was in great demand to address the Mutual Improvement Societies that abounded in the district. He spoke with authority and his words were heeded partly, I am sure, because of his style of oratory, but mainly because he had risen through the hierarchy of the mining industry from door boy to pit manager. He had been closely involved, during his thirty-four years at Talke-o'-th'-Hill, in the fearful disasters that befell the men and dogged the fortunes of that dangerous coalfield. Once I had started to read *'A Reminiscence of a Collier's Life'* I found it hard to leave. I have shown the script to a few close friends and their reaction has been the same. The characters live in the anecdotes. The senses are stirred by the vivid accounts and the descriptions of life underground. The high-flown rhetoric reflects the Primitive Methodist preaching of the Victorian era, the Wrath of God, Fire and Brimstone, Hell and Damnation, the Ranters' stock in trade. But, be not deceived, the message is sincere enough and I defy anyone not to be moved, to laughter, certainly and, probably almost to tears by what is written.

Great grandpa Lawton was rarely spoken of in my family, 'a prophet without honour in his own country,' and I learned nothing of him at all as I grew up. My grandmother, Hannah (Lawton) Irving, resembled him in both looks and character and maybe here we have the first clue as to why he featured so little in her accounts of her life. She was the youngest of his five children and showed her strength of character by marrying the man of her choice in the face of much paternal opposition. This certainly caused a rift between them and my mother and her sisters saw little of their prestigious relative. By the time they were little girls Grandpa Lawton was spoken of with something approaching reverence and it was rumoured in the family that he never darkened their door. Certainly they merit no mention among the other grandchildren at his funeral and I never knew my mother to speak of him with any affection or with any firm certainty of her facts. Her best recollection was of meeting him at Denby Station where his servant, pony and trap, awaited to transport him to one of his important meetings. They would then ride with him as far as Openwoodgate, but he never, it seems, ventured along Overlane to the family home. There, he may well have been surprised to find he had much in common with the son-in-law, Robert Armstrong Irving, he so despised. For Robert too had furthered his education by his own efforts and was a much respected employee of Denby Pottery where he held the position of Chief Designer. Reconciliation was not to be and Charles continued to prosper remote from his beloved "Nancy" to the end of his days. There was one recorded exception. On February 7th, 1920 he was among the mourners at the funeral of his grand-daughter Hilda Lawton Irving, the youngest child of Hannah and Robert who, at the tender age of sixteen years and nine months, succumbed to the scourge of the labouring classes, tuberculosis. Charles was by this time an old, old man with but one year of Grace remaining.

His fame as an expert on colliery safety spread, and much of his time was devoted to public speaking and to public service. He came to Ripley from Talke-o'-th'-Hill Colliery in Staffordshire in 1883 to be colliery manager at Messrs. Ford's Marehay Main Pits a position he held for fifteen years.

Bunker's Hill, Talke Pit 1890

Talke o' the Hill Pit 1915

13

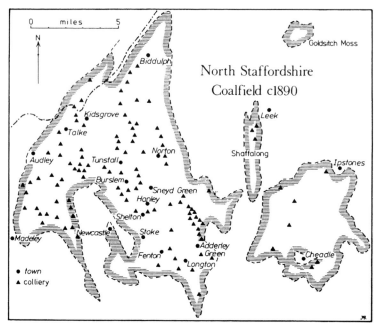

The distribution of collieries in North Staffordshire about 1800

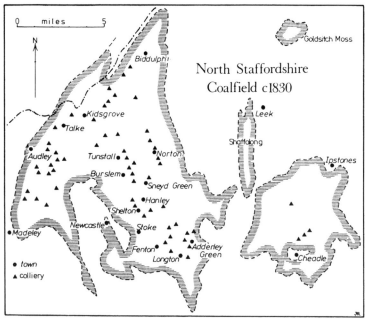

The distribution of collieries in North Staffordshire about 1830

14

CHAPTER TWO

'THE FIERY MINES OF STAFFORDSHIRE'

MAN AND COAL

Man has long had a relationship with fire. It has played a part in rituals and ceremonies, signalled approaching danger, spread good tidings, protected him from wild beasts, cooked his food and warmed his flesh. The use of coal as a fuel is comparatively recent and the 'black gold' was only recognised as a treasure when an Elizabethan statesman discovered the national asset, a 'verie soile' that the English and Scottish earth seemed to yield in more places and in greater abundance than anywhere else. The pressure on the forests from the growing European population, meant that the need for coal to support industry, both at home and abroad, became more evident, causing the Archbishop of York to say forcefully in 1685, "God bless Yorkshire, and preserve the coal-pits!" Jonathan Swift claimed that Ireland was dependent on England because she had neglected to develop coal-mines of her own. Lack of this new fuel was recognised, in the 17th century, as a serious national handicap and every continental country envied England her collieries. Discoveries of limited outcrops of coal, easily gathered from the surface led to further and deeper exploration. The first method used rods and augers to discover the whereabouts of coal. These were very poor tools in that they gave little information about the depth of the deposit or the thickness and quality of the coal, because so much dross was mixed in the samples brought to the surface. It was also impossible to learn the direction or conformation of the seam so it was difficult to determine whether or not extraction would be a viable or profitable enterprise. However, the demand for coal was such that greater and greater efforts were made to find it and to hew it from the ground. Gone, sadly, were the days when fires were fuelled with wood and turf, commodities that, like water, were free to village dwellers. Coal became a dominant item of expenditure for the impoverished householder and it was the mainstay of all burgeoning industries the world over. The unpredictability of supply caused great fluctuations in price but it was always an expensive item. It would cost a poor labourer one tenth of his annual wage to buy two or three tons. At times when the coal industry was in crisis the poor had to stand by, helpless, whilst the stewards of the landed gentry, the privileged classes, collected and carted away load after load. When the supply of coal from the north dried up many poor people in London perished for want of fuel.

There was money to be made and the landowners were not slow to exploit their assets. Staffordshire was said to be one vast coalfield. There is evidence to suggest that coal had been mined here as early as 2nd century AD. Few records exist and there seems to have been little activity until 13th century and even to the 15th century output seems to have been insignificant. The field was divided into three sections, South Staffordshire, Cannock Chase and North Staffordshire. Here, amongst others, lay Talke-o'-th'-Hill Colliery owned in Lawton's time by Thomas Kinnersley Esq, who lived at Clough Hall, and worked for him by the North Staffordshire Coal and Iron Company. The North Staffordshire mines were notoriously dangerous. They lay in folds at the south-western edge of the Pennines. The Potteries field was by far the largest in area and it had the greatest depth of workable coal but, like all the others, it was prone to flooding, enormous concentrations of gas and fiery explosions. The coal seams pitched sharply, often rising steeply and with much faulting, making the mining of this district particularly hazardous and very expensive. However the seams were of considerable size – up to ten feet thick – and of high quality hard coal and thus the mined coal was very saleable and much sought after. The fiery mines of Staffordshire were therefore regarded as an acceptable risk in terms of the rewards available.

There were no navigable rivers in this part of Staffordshire and the development of the coal industry made a pretty slow start until the advent of firstly the canals in about 1770 and then the railways. By the middle of the 19th century the full extent of Staffordshire's potential as a supplier of premium coal was being realised. The industry had grown steadily during the 18th century. It is recorded that in 1764 Thomas Poole found coal in a small piece of land at Talke that yielded him £800 in clear profit that year. Until the last quarter of the 18th century the economics of the coalfields of North Staffordshire were dependent upon the growth in demand from the pottery manufacturers. Once the Trent and Mersey canal was operational in 1777, North Staffordshire collieries entered the national economic equation. There would be rapid expansion but for some time the call for supplies came mainly from the kilns and the homes of the Potteries.

Like most extractive industries, the technology involved and the machinery and methods used were slow to develop. There were no 'great leaps forward' as in the iron and railway industries. Miners were relatively well paid and their wages included payments in kind that enabled most of the homes to have a warm hearth and regular hot food. This was a significant blessing, for the majority of labour in a cold and damp Britain, had to endure much hardship. In the 18th century most pits were using the well tried but inefficient system of 'bord and pillar' – often known as 'stall and pillar'. Along the face, some of the coal was extracted forming a chamber or 'bord' and then a pillar of coal was left, as a supporting column for the roof, between the bords. This way several colliers could work their own stalls in the face at the same time. The result was that the pillars remaining often contained more coal than was extracted. The deeper the pit the wider the pillars and the worse the extraction ratio. Clearly, once the main bords had been exhausted there was a great temptation for the miners to rob the pillars to supplement their take home pay. Robbing was often authorised by the managers to improve the extraction ratio. It was not until 1795 that a partial solution was found when 'panel working' was introduced, which allowed half of every second pillar to be removed more safely. This system was based on dividing the colliery into sections of between 10 to 20 acres each and building walls, up to 50 yards thick, of stone and waste round each section to help support the roof and to prevent major subsidence at the surface.

Generally the demand and the best price received was for coal in very large pieces. This meant that the hewer would undercut the face of the stall at floor level and use a crowbar or driven wedges to loosen the coal above. The deeper the stall was cut into the seam, the greater the risk of gas accumulation, roof falls and injury. The coal lumps would then be removed by others and transported to the pit bottom where they would be raised to the bank or pithead. Women and children often took on this duty in order to supplement the family earnings – the miner, his wife and children forming a close unit both economically and culturally. The coal was moved along the roadways in a *'corf'*, a basket and loaded into a wooden sledge or a tram to be dragged to the pit bottom. Here the corves would be hung onto the winding rope and hauled to the surface. In some instances, in older and shallower pits, women and girls would carry the corves on their backs to the surface, a painful and exhausting process for up to ten hours a day!

At the start of the operation of 'winning' a new mine the shaft was sunk to the proscribed depth and levels run to the seam. Preferably there were two shafts – the downcast shaft bringing fresh air and some distance away another parallel up-cast shaft for removal of foul air. The up-cast shaft would have a coal fired furnace at its bottom to provide the energy to drive the air upwards, forcing fresh air to be drawn into the mine. It was not until 1873 that it became law to have a minimum of two shafts serving each pit. Before that many pits had very poor ventilation as the single shaft was divided along its axis so that up-flow and down flow of air could take place. This severely restricted the space available for the winding gear transporting people, materials and coal to and from the surface and presented a further hazard in time of disaster when good clear access was critical to rescue. Sufficient rates of air movement and air change were an essential for the safe operation of a pit.

The twin dangers of gas accumulation and of flooding were ever present. The adoption in the early part of the 18th century of the thermally inefficient Newcomen atmospheric steam engine and, a little later, the improvement of steam driven pumps over the next five decades may be regarded as a rapid technological advance in the context of mining time scales. This did much to alleviate the problem of flooding but continuous operation of the pumps was a necessity. After an explosion pumping could be interrupted and rescue prevented. The technical difficulties of adequate safe ventilation awaited the availability of steam power to drive rotary fans. Electricity would provide a final solution but this would not happen until the 20th century. The introduction of the Davey Safety Lamp c.1820 was not wholly welcomed in Staffordshire because of its low level of illumination. The alarming use of candles together with the self-destructive tendency to unlock and remove lamp tops went on for some time. Collieries with good management concentrated on improving mine ventilation systems and strict adherence to safe practice. It was essential that there should be proper control of the air flow system and that fresh air in sufficient quantity was swept through the workings without short-circuiting. To this end airtight *'stoppings'*, permanent doors – usually double doors to form an airlock – were used to prevent any leakage when *'trams'* of corves went through to the pit bottom. Temporary doors called *'brattices'*, curtains of impregnated sackcloth, were used to control the airflow close to the working face. Young boys, 10 to 12 years old, were employed to open and close these doors and prevent the build up of foul air and dangerous gas. Thus the safety of a whole level often depended on the awareness of a mere child!

The colliery at Talke, which opened c.1850, was likely to have been mined by the *'longwall'* system that was more common in Staffordshire at this time. This gave a much better recovery ratio but possibly increased the danger of explosion due to the increase in the scale of the operation. Longwall mining meant that the face of the coal seam was cut away along its length, the roof being supported close to the face with wooden pit props. The face was *'holed'* being cut to a given depth, usually 20 – 40 inches either, undercut by hand or, holed and loosened by firing *'shots'* – powder cartridges. After removal of the section of cut coal, the props were moved forward to the face and the process repeated. The roof was allowed to fall naturally some distance behind the working face, a dangerous area known as the *'gob'* or *'goaf'*. Where there were thick seams, this area was packed with stone and rubbish to minimise the effect of subsidence at the surface and to allow space for the 'gates', the roadways giving access to move the cut coal to the pit bottom. In Staffordshire the fiery nature of some mines with long faces sometimes required a modified system, a combination of stall and pillar with longwall. The working area was divided into sections and separated by 'fire ribs', solid walls of unworked coal with small accesses to allow the transport of coal to the roadways. As each subsection was worked out it was sealed up to isolate any gas pockets.

'The Fiery Mines of Staffordshire'

In time, the larger pits would divide the working process into individual functions so that the separate activities were each carried out by specialists. Only the colliers would hew the coal at the face assisted perhaps by his journeyman, his *'marrow'*. At the end of their stint they were free to go. The operation of loosening the coal from the face into very big sections, often of several tons each and, the subsequent breaking of these into portable blocks, was done by *'hammer-men'*, *'rivers'* and *'remblers'*. Transport to the pit bottom and thence to the bank was for other specialists, such as *'hurriers'* and *'hookers-on'*. Thus the working group formed a close knit team, able to work as an entity and which was exploitable by an entrepreneur. This co-operative was developed into a self-employed unit and was known as the *'butty system'*. The *'butty'* often with his relatives as partners, would contract with the colliery manager to carry out, for an agreed price, all the relevant work involved. He supplied the labour, horses, materials, equipment and supervision to get the coal and make good the pit. Inevitably this led to exploitation of his workforce and was very unpopular with the miners and their families. Greedy contractors working on limited capital were a sure recipe for much injury, loss of life and the many mine disasters that should never have been recorded as accidents.

The social history of mining in Staffordshire followed the general pattern. It is hard for us to believe now that as recently as the early days of the 19th century children as young as four or five were taken underground with their parents to spend twelve hours crouched in an alcove, seated on the damp coal. These little mites were known as *'trappers'*. They held a piece of string that was attached to a *'brattice'*, an air-door, and when they heard a wagon approach they pulled the string and opened the door to let it pass through. These wagons would, in all probability, be pushed or pulled by women or young girls, many as young as thirteen. The colliers, hewing at the coal-face, used these women to help load the coal they had extracted and haul it to the bank to be lifted to the surface. They were called *'hurriers'* and not without good reason as they were responsible for getting the collier's quota of coal away from his place. If he fell short his pay would be reduced so he was not averse to using verbal and physical abuse on any *'hurrier'* who couldn't keep up with him. The women had to crawl on hands and knees with a harness over their shoulders, the tail going between their legs to attach to the loaded wagon that was often not on wheels but on runners similar to those of a sledge. Usually they worked naked to the waist and reports tell of men, working naked alongside them, being aroused at the sight and sounds of the sweating, panting females to the point where sexual intercourse took place with the result that, as one report puts it *'many bastards were born'*.

It was not until 1842 that this degrading and inhuman exploitation of women and children was brought to an end following the report of the Commission set up to investigate the whole issue of the employment of women and children underground. The proprietors had also by this time realised that horses were cheaper and stronger so they raised no objection to the new legislation. The objection came, strangely enough, from the women themselves who relied on their wages and the money brought home by their children to maintain a decent standard of living for the family, and from the men. Their objection was not in any way based on moral grounds, oh no! *They* complained that women who worked down the pit never learned how to sew, mend a shirt or cook and so made very unsatisfactory wives! There is a story of one man, father of seven whose six daughters, the oldest eighteen years of age, all worked with him underground and he was waiting eagerly for his little boy to join them! There are many tales of debauchery, incest and bestiality. These practices were not confined to English pits. Emile Zola in his novel 'Germinal' wrote movingly of similar conditions in the coal-mines of France. Charles Lawton was well aware of this almost sub-human culture and he lobbied hard for the changes that came about in 1872 when all pits came under strict government control. Still, the Government Inspectors' Report of 1878 found that there were boys aged ten and twelve working underground and many women doing very arduous and menial tasks of grading and sorting coal at the pithead. In fact these poor creatures had become something of a tourist attraction many visitors coming to watch them at work in their men's clothes and totally blackened by coal dust. Postcards depicting them were on sale in local shops and it was only when the press of visitors threatened to impede the operations and reduce the work rate that the proprietors closed the pit gates to visitors. Change was gradual but it was happening. Safety was improving but it was still a fact that a collier's job in North Staffordshire was not for the faint hearted.

CHAPTER THREE

'A Reminiscence of a Collier's Life'
by
Charles Lawton

We have often met to listen to the thriling adventures of far famed travelers, who have gone forth into the most desolate places and into the wildest regions. Who have penetrated into the most dense forests — and have rode upon the wildest and most stormy seas — Who have for a time associated with the most rude and uncultivated Savages and very barely escaped the greed of the most Barbourous Canabals — Gone forth with Scientific aims & for the spread of Civilization.

And we have met before now to listen to the recital of the startling deeds of Red plumed warriors — Who have gone forth against the greatest odds — under the hottest fire of foreign Soldiery — amid the hail of Iron and the shower of Blood — Who have been Brave unto Death for their Country's weal and for their Social Rights. We have also met before now on past occasions to hear the story of Gods Mayrtd Host — who have pined in the cell Hung at the gibbet or Burned at the Stake — for Conciense and for Religion. Our story tonight lays no claim to mighty deed or to famous feats of any kind.

The story of a flannel coated clog shod collier can not by any means be of any great public interest — His travels are out of sight in the Dens Caves and Culverts of a mine — and being so far out of sight he is so far out of mind, and our only apology — (if an apology is needed) is a faint and feeble attempt to break the silence that surrounds the Collier's lot — I have

'A Reminiscence of a Collier's Life'

often wondered dear Sir why as a class — no poets sing of us
— Why no painter takes us to his canvas and gives us life —
Why does no sculpturers chisel immortalize the miners calling
— Why does no favourite author give us a record on the pages
of our country's History — I look amongst the Literature of
the times — and amongst the monuments that adorn our public
parks — and amongst the Galleries of Celebrated painters, and
I ask where is the Collier — And echo replies Where

I maintain Dear Sir that a collier's life is not without Heroism
— nor his Home without Poetry — nor are the incidents of
many a colliers life less interesting than those that command
the attentions of many a newspaper Special.

One reason why we are so unnoticed may be that we are so
difficult of access. There are special correspondents that will
be in their glory in the trenches before Sebastopol — or
scaling the walls of the Malekoff but would tremble from top
to toe at the idea of going down a coal mine — swinging at the
end of a rope one inch thick with 200 yards of darkness below
their feet is a feat they put of as the last thing they shall
ever try at.

I have seen the man that could fight a pack of Russian wolves
like a madman -- who could travel thousands of miles over
Siberian snow — who confessed he did not like the idea of
going down a pit — I have conversed with the man whose
travels have fetched 20/- per volume who said that a coal pit
was the last place he should visit.

'A Reminiscence of a Collier's Life'

Men who never could be called cowards have leaned over the fence rail at the pit top and have looked down for about 6 yards and drawn back with a shudder have said "Aye I shouldn't go down for the world" — and this being so we can scarcely wonder if the collier is and remains out of sight and out of the Public mind. But the collier has to fight a battle — to fight as pluckily — as bravely — as any red-coated soldier on martial plains with difficulties and danger around him more appaling. He fights not for months to return into peaceful abodes of rest. He fights year in year out. He fights for his daily crust to keep the wolf from his door to keep the bailiff from his home — to keep the shoes on his childrens feet to keep the little pictures on his walls — to keep decent attire on his wife and to keep the roses on the cheeks of his children — and if he can do this honestly and fully and continually he gains Victory more glorious than many who have strained the annals of earth. His medals of Honour he carries with him to the grave in the form of scars and blue Stains in his flesh.

And Where is the Colliers Battlefeild

Is it on Waterloo or on some plain were the carnage has made the red soil verdant with vegetable life. No! It is amid the Darkness and Gloom of a Coal mine. In a land where the Sun never Shines — where the Moon never sheds her silvery beams — where the stars never twinkle — where the birds never sing — where flocks and herds never feed — where trees never blossom — where flowers never bloom — where the hills show no verdure — where the valleys are never green — where the skies are never blue — where the horizon shows no gold —

25

'A Reminiscence of a Collier's Life'

where childhood never plays — where infancy never smiles — in an atmosphere that is never pure — in a night that knows no morning — in a living Tomb — with a firmament of rock — with an horizon of coal 200 hundred fathoms below the tread of human foot is the Colliers Battlefield. The implements of his warfare are very carnal indeed. Half a doz. picks — a set of punching tools — a hammer and a wedge a spade a hopper — with these he fights and wins a glorious noble victory.

May I ask Mr. C. why the mechanical trades of this country have taught their sons to look down at the calling of the collier as one infinitely below their station and as one that requires very little brains or skill. I contend that such an idea is a great mistake. There is no trade of more commercial value to the nation and there is no calling where skill and courage can be better employed. A mechanic may be alright at a bench where he has served an apprenticeship — but if he were put into some of our stalls he whould be a dead man in an hour and all near him whould run a great risk. Every man to his trade and let none be held in contempt. Show me the mechanic who can carry a candle in the levil without getting in the dark — show me the mechanic who knows how to stick a candle up — show me the mechanic who knows how to snuff a candle without burning his fingers — show me the mechanic that can walk without getting in the gutter — or one that can tell whether he is going up the pit or down — or one that can tell a straight tale as to the way he went when he got out of the cage or could walk without knocking his head. But it is not only the mechanic that has looked down at the collier.

'A Reminiscence of a Collier's Life'

All along the past the collier has been held in very low esteem. In the year 1859 Sir Thomas Smith wrote a record of all the trades in England but would not enter the colliers. In the year 1739 Southey says "The colliers are a class of men as lawless as the foresters and far more brutal". 100 years ago another author says "These unhappy wretches seldom see the light of the sun. They are buried in the bowels of the earth without the least sign of improvement. They live on the worst of food and breathe air so poisoned as to make it a living tomb". 100 years ago the collier could not leave his place of work if he wanted — like a serf he was a part of the concern and was transfered to the next owner by the powers of the lease

King Charles II made a law to forbid colliers getting as much wages as ordinary labourers and the same law made it imperitive that they should work every day. Negroes were free men in England before the collier. But Sir there is at work a mighty power with a mighty voice. A voice that makes all tyrants tremble — a power that shakes the throne of Empires — a power that grows and spreads and climbs high and goes down deep. The power and the voice I refer to is Public Opinion in the last half of the 18th century — in the first half of the present century Public Opinion was muzzled, gagged and fettered. But today Public Opinion is on the side of industry — call that industry by what name ye will. And the voice of Public Opinion has spoken out with a trumpets voice saying — The man who produces for his country the source of its greatest wealth — that produces for every home its greatest luxury deserves the esteem of all his countrymen — and he shall have

'A Reminiscence of a Collier's Life'

a seat in his country's Parliment and shall help in making his country's laws.

Public Opinion has been on a visit to the colliers cottage and has come to the conclusion that the colliers wife is as much a woman as Queen Victoria is one and that is capable of womanly instincts and a mothers love and the voice of Public Opinion has spoken out with a trumpet voice and said — "The colliers wife and the colliers daughter shall no longer go into the mines to be degraded and abused by their lords and masters worse than ordinary beasts of burden." Each one shall be Queen of a little domain and shall by her almost angelic influence add to the charms and the happiness of the far famed homes of England. And what has Public Opinion done for the colliers Child listen to Mrs. Browning just over fifty years ago — what does she say

The young lambs are bleating in the meadows
The young birds are chirping in their nests
The young fawns are playing with the shadows
The young flowers are blowing towards the west
But the young, young children. Oh my brothers
They are weeping bitterly
Weeping in the playtime of the others
In the country of the free
Go out children from the mines and from the city
Sing out children as the little thrushes do
Pluck your handfulls of the meadow cowslips pretty
Laugh aloud to feel your fingers let them through
But they answer — Are your cowslip of the meadows

'A Reminiscence of a Collier's Life'

Like our weeds anear the mine
Leave us quiet in the dark of the coal shadows
From your pleasures fair and fine

For — Oh said the children we are weary
For we cannot run or leap
If we cared for any meadows it were merely
To droop on them and sleep
Our knees are trembling sorely in the stooping
We fall upon our faces as we go
And underneath our heavy eyelids drooping
The fairest flowers would seem as pale as snow

For all day long we our burden bearing
Through the coal dark underground
Or all day long we drive the weels of iron
In the factories round and round
Still all the day the iron weels go round
Grinding life down from its mark
And the childrens souls that God is calling sunward
Spin on blindly in the dark

How long! How long! Oh cruel nation
Will you stand to move the world upon a childs heart
Stiffle down with nailed heel its palpitation
And head onward to the throne amid the mark
Our blood splashes upward. O gold heaper
And our purple shows your path
And the childs sob in the silence curses deeper
Than the strong man in his wrath.

'A Reminiscence of a Collier's Life'

If I go Sir from this platform and shout down every pit in the kingdom and ask them to send the women and children up they will call up in return and tell me there is not any down. If I collect all the colliery managers in the kingdom on this platform and I ask "You that are in favour of taking women and children into the pits again show your right hand". No hand whould be held up. I might summon all the colliery owners in the kingdom here and ask all you that are in favour of employing women and children in the mines again shew up — Not a single hand whould go and if one should forego the infamy and lift his hand I think the leproseys of Gehazi whould cleave unto it.

You and I Sir can scarcely be called old men yet but we have lived in wonderful times when change has followed change — and law as followed law — and invention has followed invention — with a rapidity the world before time never dreamed of and if the men of the so-call'd 'good old times' where here today they whould not know themselves.

We are only of yesterday but we have lived in stirring times. We have come into the world in time to see the benefits made by the repeal of the Corn Laws. We have seen the English Cotton Factories pass through a complete transition by the inventions of Arkwright, Hargreaves and Compton. We have seen the tailoring trades and the shoemaking trades completely revolutionised by the invention of the sewing machine which was patented so late as 1858. We have seen the

'A Reminiscence of a Collier's Life'

co-operative system grow into vast proportions and large pondourous concerns are in operation employing thousands of thousands of hands and who have invested millons of pounds under the name of Limited Liability Companies — and who are today opening Commercial Enterprise the whole world over.

We have seen the Old Pickford Fly Boat once the pride of the canals pass out of repute and today it is as little thought of as poor old James Brindley who lies unhonoured in Newchapel churchyard. We have seen the last red and yellow old stage coach go rumbling along (down the Red Bull Bank). We have heard the coachmans horn blow its last note. We have seen all the old Raw Bone Engines sold for scrap iron and all the old hemp ropes cut up for pitch rope. We have seen all the Gin Horses sold to the Tanyard and all the old wooden corves sold for firewood.

We have seen the famous collieries of 20 tons per day grow into concerns of 1000 tons per day having a wage bill of over £1000 per week We have seen energetic boys without influencial parentage or the advantages of wealth step up the ladder of Prosperity untill they have become the Coal Kings and the Iron Kings of our day. And we see today a wider market for Intelligence, Industry and for good moral business young men than ever the world offered before.

Well Sir, I am a Collier Born in a colliers village and raised in a colliers cottage and allmost naturally when a child I looked forward with high anticipation to the time when I should have

'A Reminiscence of a Collier's Life'

a flannel jacket a pair of clogs and a hat with a piece of candle stuck in it and wear Black face.

I became a Mining Engineer when only 6 years of age. I sunk a pit in my mothers garden 36" deep and 12" wide. I had a weelbarrow trundle for an engine an apple tree bough for pit frame. I wound many a day until my pit sides fell in and then I liquidated.

The first time I went down a pit was against my will. I was 7 years of age and having taken breakfast to a sinking pit I stopped to look on. The banksman was a rude senseless fellow and takeing hold of me he held me over the pit, head downwards. He then put me into the hopper and sent me down the shaft. At the bottom a man poured a bucket of very dirty water over me and used very unparlimentary language, he charged me with hindering the work, like Joseph's Brothers they held a confab what must be done with me. One suggested filling me in the bottom of a Bowk. If we send him up said one he will fall out before he gets to the top, and KILL SOME OF US so they called to the Banksman to send a lashing chain down. They then made me promise I whould not come down again and then took the chain, passed it under my arms in a running noose with the ring between my shoulders and with my arms and legs hanging loose I was sent up the pit post fashion and from the bungling way the banksman landed me at the top the wonder is that I did not fall down again. But my Father has taken care of me when no one else could.

'A Reminiscence of a Collier's Life'

I became a pit Boy in real earnest in the then colliery village of Kidsgrove which was preaphs the most important Coal and Iron works in North Staffordshire. And I will give you a few of my earliest recollections of that time. It was the property of Thomas Kinnersley of Clough Hall. He rode around the works on an Iron Grey pony and had very bad habit of being there just when he wasn't wanted. He carried a long whip — the lash was just 6 feet long. I remember it quite well, so does many another Old Kidsgrove Boy. He was followed by a footman in livery riding on a Brown Cob and behind him came a large mastif dog. I think the master could beat the mastif at growling and he used to growl out, "If ever you meet a lad, thrash him. If he does not deserve it now, he will do".Thomas Kinnersley sleeps with his fathers in Ashley Church and when you visit his tomb tread softly and don't wake him up.

His General Manager was Mr. Robert Heath Senr. Old Bobby everybody called him. He was a rather humourous and excentric old man, and much respected by the men. He had nearly everybody's good word. Kidsgrove mourned for him when he died. The next in authority was Mr. Robert Heath Junr. He was always called Young Bobby. He was a young very genteel looking man, full of pluck energy and determination. He whould admit of no obstacles in his way — if it were only a piece of coal he whould kick it 20 yards before him. He talked loudly to himself as he went along and drew plans on the ground with his boot toe — people said he was soft. I had the misfortune to meet him one day in a narrow passage in the Boiler yard I though he whould push past me — but no. With

'A Reminiscence of a Collier's Life'

his open hand he made my cheek burn all that day and I blushed on that side of my face for a week.

The Colliery Bailiff was a tall old gentleman. His name was James Mellor. He was only known as "Jemmy Luke". He wore a long flannel jacket winter and summer that reached down to his heels and carried a long walking stick. He was very religious was old Jemmy and he often told us lads to be good and not forget to say our prayers. But we did not quite understand his religion at times. If we did not keep the pit on he whould send for the Butty up, and he whould get into a rage and hit the ground with his stick and he whould say,"There wants more Devil amongst them lads — never be any stuff out of this pit till there's more Devil in it".

There was a thick-set jolly fellow for Engineer his name was Joseph Mayer. He built the Speedwell and Valentine engines. Time whould fail me Sir to tell of all the worthies I then knew, of Tadpole, the Dog Fighter, of Old Clogger Rowley the Antiquarian, of Good Sam Sims the Methodist, of Sammy Sambrook the poet, of old Israel the chimney sweep, of the Rev. F Wade the vicar, of Jolly Jesse Bedson the Clerk, of Old William Thomas the friend of Mr. Kinnersley and the Duke of Wellington and a host of others who obtained a name for themselves amongst the common people of Kidsgrove and who lived like they died and now rest in peace.

There was one, Sir, whose name I have not mentioned and to whom I shall call special attention. He was the foreman at the workshops. He had possessed a very inventive mind and been a

'A Reminiscence of a Collier's Life'

useful servant to his master but the time of which I speak he was getting old and infirm. His proper name was John Gates but people always called him John Boge — a name he allways hated. He had invented a Signal Bell that was in use at the Bomb Shell Engine, and some wicked wit made a song about it which began with

"Old John Boge He worked a dodge all people to exell
He nailed a clock unto a block
To ring the Bomb Shell Bell."

I was sent to the shops one day to get a Bank hook repaired and the man who sent me told me that I must not forget my manners. So I went very gaily up to this gentleman who I found in the stores emptying an old cask. I remember his hands were covered with Black looking oil. I said, "If you please Mr. Boge will you tell me who must piece me this hook?" That Black greasy hand came across my cheek in no time and something like sparks came out of my eyes. "I'll give you Boge," he said. I did not know his proper name and I wondered what was up. Old Robinson the shoeing smith saw me crying and he called me to him and asked me what was up. He then said I must not call him Boge but must go again and call him Mr. Gates so I again went up within a few yards of him and said, "Please Mr. Gates who must piece me this?" He said in reply, "Luke Keen". I was in a muddle. I asked him again, he again said, or rather shouted, "Look Keen" and he said if I came any more he whould serve my other cheek the same. So I came along the yard crying and I did not know what to do. Old Robinson called me again and I told him that I could not piece

35

'A Reminiscence of a Collier's Life'

it. Mr. Gates had told me to be sharp over it. Poor old Robinson saw through it and I wondered what on earth he could see to laugh at and he said he did not mean that you must be sharp. But there is a blacksmith at yonder hearth who does such jobs. His name is Luke Keen. Take it to him.

Amongst the Butties there were stars of less magnitude but all of them remarkable men in their way. I may mention The Bainbridges, The Potts, The Baileys, The Knappers, The Lawtons including Old Beardy Lawton of Newchapel, the famous Cock fighter, Cartledge Lovatt and James Lucas, now President of the North Staffordshire Mining and Mechanical Engineers. Head Butties were known from under Butties because they carried their 2 thumbs into their armhole and the under Butties only carried one so.

I did not begin to work in the pits quite so early as other boys. I was 10 years of age. I had previously worked on the Bank and at the forge.

And now I will tell you how I found things below ground when I began to work as pony driver at Kidsgrove and I must ask you to come with me a day below in fancy and I will try to instruct you a little. You must be out of bed by four o' clock as we go down at half past five and you will want with you a big dinner because it is often eight before we get out at night. Everybody is by stents and the stents are made to be finished at 6 o'clock with about five minutes out for meals if all goes on straightforward, but as hindrances occur it is often 7 and 8 before the pony drivers have done. To walk from Butt Lane to the pit is two miles and then there is a mile to go below the surface.

Going up through Kidsgrove Village we hear at half past four the tramp of hundreds of clogs and voices at every pitch are calling somebody at every door they pass. We see in the distance great bonfires which shew us the possitions of the different pits, ours is No.10. we get to the pit top to find others there before us. Some have been there since four o'clock for the Butties have a rule that answers well for them they who come first go down first and he who is first can ride along all the rest must tramp it.

The Old Engine begins to move and we draw up around the pit top in lines. 4 men and a boy get into the corf and two more step onto the carraige until our turn comes. We get to the bottom just in time to hear Bob the far end pony start in so all who come down now must walk. We must go to the Candle Box for our candles and seated on an empty tub you see Mr. Head Butty. He looks at every body savage and speaks sharp to the men and promises all the lads a taste of his strap. You can hear him 20 yards away as he says to the men and boys as they pass, "Where ast bin till naw. Dost know what time it is. Thee must keep thy Bottomer on today or thee must come out. Now then sharpen off along. I'll be after thee just now." The men come down and form into a line for a march to the far end you can see a long row of lights and the colliers have to carry with them five or six picks each and a pound of candles hang from his waist. He has on his back a big flannel jacket and in his pockets his dinner and bottle. His picks are stuck under

'A Reminiscence of a Collier's Life'

one arm, he has a pick head upwards for a walking stick, his candle he sticks between his fingers. The roads these men have to travel are very low, not 5 feet high so he must stoop or tip his head. The rails are buried in mud or water for four inches and he must pick his way on the top of the rail for a distance of 1000 yards a feat worthy of Blondin the great rope walker for should he slip of the rail he will go up to the middle of the leg in mud. Tramp! Tramp! Tramp! Splash! Splash! Splash! on they go as persperation rolls of them every limb aches with the painful march by the time they reach the far end siding. But as yet only a part of their task is done. They must climb the dips to a distance of about 400 yards. To do this the colliers stick their picks down their jacket backs and lay hold of a chain. They pull themselves up hand o'er hand for the dips rise at an angle of 40 to 45 degrees. It is now near 6 o'clock but not one of them has begun his days work yet. The long painful march counts nothing towards his wages though many a tradesman whould think it a big days work of itself. Having reached the top they throw of their flannels and only keep on their trousers and caps. They certainly are a queer looking group — part European and part Negro. They only washed face and hands last night.

Colliers as a rule are a cheerfull class of men, none more so and preaphs on many subjects behond that of their own calling they may be termed ignorant. But no class of men work harder, and very few trades work as hard. We will follow that man into his place and we shall see if what we say is true. At the time of which I am speaking every man examined his own place and no records were kept. So we see him going forward

'A Reminiscence of a Collier's Life'

holding his candle shaded by his hand near to the roof trying to find Sulphur. He finds a bit near his face, lies flat down sticks his candle on his pick shaft, lights it and off it goes. He now takes his pick and knocks on the roof and on the sides — and no musician can find a discord sooner, nor can an Indian Chief smell danger so far off as can an old practised collier. He knows that a little error in judgment in these matters may cost him his life. So he takes a prop and puts it to the tender part and then he proceeds to pull out the bowels of the earth — out bit by bit. He sticks up his candle on the nearest prop and he kneels on one knee, then on both knees, sits on the cross head of his pick, lies on one side, then on the other side, now on his belly, then on his back. Now cramped up in a ball like possition his pick keeps proper time 60 strokes per minute and the air thickens with the blackest of all dust. Nothing can now be seen of him but the whites of his eyes or his teeth. His candle is scarcely visible yet he never pauses and the place becomes hotter and his limbs are bathed in persperation. The dust is so thick now that you cannot see him at all. You can hear him trying to sing a song keeping time with his pick.

> "Was there ever so slaveing or slashing a trade
> Such a trade as this terrible hewing
> I wish I'd been born to the plough or the spade
> To Building or Bakeing or Brewing
> I'm up in the morning before it is light
> And down in the pit in the dark
> And if I get up before it is night
> I'm asleep from my terrible "wark"
> I'm making the ladies and gentlemen warm

39

'A Reminiscence of a Collier's Life'

Though I ain't got no latin or learning
I get them their coals for winter and storm
But they don't think of me while they're burning."

I must now call your attention to the "Bottomer". Who gave him that name I don't know. If I had been his God-Father I should have called him the "Man-Ass". He does the work of a man and a horse. He fills the coals from the collier and draws them away to the dip then runs with them part way down the dip. He uses more strength than a collier and works longer hours. He wore tracings like a horse which goes over his shoulders and down his back terminating in a tail or draw chain. These tracings are called by the ominous name of the "Bite". I don't know who invented it but it is an instrument of torture that ought to be put in the British Museum — as a relic of a barbourous age. I would put it in a case with the Gibbet, The Rack and the Thumbscrew of the Spanish Inquisition. You may think I am hard on the Bite. I am — It has been hard on me. I have suffered much in many ways. I have had bleeding hands from cracks made by the frost. I have had bleeding feet from ulcerated wounds caused by tramping all the day in carry water. I have blistered hands from useing the pick and I have been scorched by the flames from gas and cut by the falling coals, but from all of these I have recovered but from the effects of the Bite I shall never recover. But for it I might have been as straight in my limbs and as strong in my lungs as some of you. My dear Mother has cried while she has dressed my raw shoulders with salt to make them hard. I speak tonight privately to all young men who value straight limbs to beware of the Bite. Just look at

'A Reminiscence of a Collier's Life'

the Kidsgrove Bottomer who crawls Toad Fashion 12 or 13 hours per day drawing a pony load behind him simply because it is not convenient height to take a pony. At the time of which I speak there was an infant race of Bottomers called "Duck Jinners", boys from 9 to 12 years of age who did the same kind of work where the roads were too small for the men to go.

One of our Bishops put a question to Uncle Tom to this effect. At what University did you graduate Mr. Henson. The poor old Blakman replied "At the University of Adversity Sir". If we were asked the question today we should have to reply "At the University of Hardwork" for I have graduated through all the stages. I am now talking about from Door tenter to Manager . And I am speaking of times when the climbing scale was more regular than it is now, for instance a young man could seldom get in for a colliers place until he had been for some time a Bottomer. And the rule was that the youngest collier took the place of any Bottomer who stayed from work odd days, but it was difficult to get a collier put under the Bite in any circumstances. In case of any dispute the one who refused was fined 6 pence which was paid to the man who took the Bite. I will give you a story that will illustrate my statements

Amongst the worthies I have named was one old Butty named Thomas Worthington. "Old Tom" he was always called because he was in his younger days and even in old age one of the most tyranncal of men. He had been a Butty a many years and had made a fortune and for a time he gave up work but in old age he took a pit and taking some of his relations in with him he

'A Reminiscence of a Collier's Life'

began Buttying again and was to be seen every morning at about 3 o'clock trudgeing of to work, and the first thing when he got to the pit was to begin to growl out "Niver seed like i my life. Noby come yet".

When the Engine man come early to get up steam he let Old Tom down the pit with the man who fed the horses. He whould open up the candle box door and sit waiting till his patience was exhausted, and then he whould go to the pit bottom and shout up, "Are you coming down todey". He had a very senatorian voice, his lung power was wonderfull he could talk about as loud as an ordinary man could shout. He had a crooked finger on his right hand with he pointed and concluded his remarks with "Mark That". And when the first ropefull came down about 5 o'clock he whould roar out "wee'n ye bin till naw aye. Golden Hill Rules is it.[1] They were going work Kidscrew when I come only give yo three quarters for today. Mark That". Well Congleton May Fair came round and all his Bottomers "Bobbed in the Hat" and all the colliers were down before they percieved that the Bottomers were missing. They also wanted to go to May Fair and all agreed that they would not take the Bottomers places. When they got up the dips the Under Butties could not get any of them to put the straps on. Meantime somebody told Old Tom that the Bottomers were not come. He roared out "Well we can do without them conner we. It's o'er if we conner do without a Bottomer. Kidscrew can do without a Bottomer yet Mark That." In a short time he was

---

[1] 'Golden Hill Rules' refers to the time when economics had forced up wages and it was possible at that North Staffs colliery for miners to live well by working only four days in the week and enjoy the leisure of the remaining days.

at the bottom of one of the dips shouting up "Are ye going begin todey. Are ye all gone sleep What dost sey. Dost sey Nobody at bottom. Didst sey as nobody at bottom. Well wait a bit till I come up an I'll see who'll bottom Mark That" He reached the top of the dips panting for breath and wipeing the sweat of he said , "I – I – I say Tom — Thee must Bottom." Tom replied that his back was bad he couldn't. Worthington roared out "we can do without Thee Kidscrew can always do without a man like thee Mark That." " Naw George Tha man Bottom 6 pence extra for thee that ha done by collier time." George said he had sprained his ankle He could not Bottom. "Tha't a idle scamp" said Old Tom "Tha shat niver wock another dey on Kidscrew ground Mark That." "Sam, Sam" shouted Old Tom. A voice from one of the headings below answered "Halloa!" "Come here, Sam." Sam came and Old Tom said "Kidscrew's come to summat Sam. A lot o' idle scamps here wonner Bottom. But theet Bottom Sam. A shillin a day extra Sam." Sam said he'd got the reumatic. Old Tom raged like a Bull in a net. He vowed he have 'em all before Mr. Heath before they struck another blow. He tried them all but one and they had all something matter they could not Bottom. His only hope was in one more. So he began to coax him. "Tell thee what Pearson — thee art the best Bottomer ever trod Kidscrew ground. I've told the lot on 'em so many a time. Tha canst always get done by collier time tha canst lick the lot of 'em and tha can do it todey. Come and put straps on an' I'll push thy in an' load one or two for thee, Mark That."

Pearson laid aside his pick and went to the Bite, took off his shirt which was a signal for the colliers to go to their work. No

43

'A Reminiscence of a Collier's Life'

chance of a play day if he was going to Bottom, and they were all very sulky over it. When Old Tom saw Pearson go to the corf he shouted "Here the man as can Bottom. He has not an idle bone in him nor iver had an' i've known him sin he were a chilt. An' knowed he Bottom if I axed him. Now Pearson look to and I'll push thee in" and he stuck his candle behind the corf and began to push. After pushing it a few yards he said "Art pulling any Pearson." "Pulling aye" said Pearson "Yore pushing none." "Well go on lad" said Tom and the old man pushed again with all his might and hearing the chain rattle he suspected that Pearson was not pulling, so he got his candle and looked over the corf where Lo! Pearson was on all fours just crawling along with his legs through the Bite straps instead of his arms. When Old Tom saw this he roared louder than ever, "Well tha't do. Theet niver dee thee wokner. Ye may all go out it o'er wi' Kickcrew ! It o'er wi' Kickcrew! it o'er wi' Kickcrew Mark That."

Time whould fail me to tell you of the way things were done through even one day's work. How men worked like Transports for 3 shillings and 2 pence per day on one meal a day. How that meal was covered by "migins" and the best parts eaten away with rats. How Rats swarmed every where. How Black Damp percolated until it was impossible to keep lights burning. How boys were thrashed and kicked by the Butties for everything that went wrong. How the Bottomers thrashed them if they did not cheat in the count and how the Butties thrashed them if they did cheat. How they were left in the pit to wash their horses after everybody else had gone up. How the Engine man whould go home to get his supper and then come again to pull

'A Reminiscence of a Collier's Life'

them out. I need not tell you how under these circumstances I have crawled home with bleeding ulcerated feet and how in the winter night the carry water has frozen on my stockings and trousers until they whould not bend. How at times I have been without food for 15 hours when the rats have eaten my dinner. How when the nights were finer I with other lads have lain in the fields and from sheer weariness have gone to sleep till someone has come to look after us and they have found us there.

I need not tell you of the imoral state of things at that time. When I tell you that in 200 men and boys in my pit there was not one that proffessed Religion and every pit in Kidsgrove had …its champion pugilist, Dog fighter, Cockfighter, Card player, Prison Bar player, Race runner and domino player, and their talk the day through was of these and of filthier things.

One great Institution at the time was the Reconning Monday. A sort of Donny Brook Fair day that reached from The Red Bull to Burslem. Wages were paid once per month at the public houses and the Monday that followed the pay was a general holliday, and those who had money to draw could, if they wished it, have a spree, and he who could not "go in" for something lively on a Reconning Monday was considered a great flat. Matches of all sorts came of that day and sights of the most disgracefull character were seen. In the evening dozens of Battles were fought at some of the Publics and women whould back their husbands, holding them on their knees and sponging them as per Ring rule. A swell prize fight by a champion at 6 o'clock in the morning whould often open the

'A Reminiscence of a Collier's Life'

day's proceedings at which hundreds whould be present and pit lads had their champion fights and these were supported by the men.

From Door boy to Collier I spent in the Kidsgrove pits and saw several reforms which I will not stop to name.Just before leaving Kidsgrove Pits I had my first Experiance of a colliery explosion. I mean now the one that occured at the Woodshutts Colliery. The day after the one at Lund Hill. I was at home when the first report was heard like the sound of a cannon and living only two fields from the pit I ran across at once to the pit bank. The force of the explosion had disarranged the timbers on top of the pit frame and a black cloud was coming up the upcast pit near the Millstone Inn. The Butt Lane and New Road folks were coming in every direction. A signal was given on the rods from the bottom which told somebody was alive and wanted to come up. James Stubbs ran up the pit frames and threw away the loose planks. In five minutes afterwards those pit frames were sent flying in the air. The wagon was sent away down from the top and fortunately no-one was bold enough to get in it. Had anyone done so I verily believe I should have joined them as I stood against the fence rail willing almost to do anything, but no-one got in. The wagon had not reached more than half way down when an awful explosion took place which for force has scarcely been equaled in this neighbourhood of explosions.

At the moment I was at the fence rail at the pit top. There was a terrific report heard for four miles and the descending wagon rope pit frames and pullies were carried away like chaff. The whole air was darkened by the dirt and material brought up the pit shaft for some minutes and the pit top on which I had stood was bellied out by the force and wagon and framework carried away.

Under such circumstances it is scarcely credible that I should have escaped injury, especially as there were so many severely cut and wounded. In fact the whole place in ten minutes looked like a battlefield. My escape was in the course of Providence and some would say it was a miracle. I was knocked or fell back in the cabin doorway which was six feet behind me and was for a minute or so stunned by a blow on my head which prevented me rising to my feet again. Meantime something came down on the roof of the cabin crashing it in I was protected from a shower of Bricks coal and timber that poured round me like a tremendous hail. For a bit I lay still as it was impossible for me to tell where I was. I had at that moment a strange fancy I thought I saw along the crut two men with two lights and they were asking me the way out. I thought much of this afterwards when it was found that there were two men still alive. As I became clear in my mind I felt at my legs and found them all right and tried to creep out but it was yet too dark. It became a little light and I crawled out and ran I did not know where and fell in the Stage hole where carts were loaded. I ran again and fell into a clay hole where lay Richard Hazlehurst. I said to him, Come on thou wilt get killed. See bricks are falling. He groaned and said, I am fast. Look at my leg, and the poor fellows leg was broke and knocked into the clay. I tried to move him further away but he could not bear to be moved, so I had to run on and get help but there were many that had to be helped home.

'A Reminiscence of a Collier's Life'

But this did not complete the calamities of that day. Late in the evening an attempt was made to let a rope down the Water pit to reach the men if any were living, and by this time thousands of people were present and the pit bank was crowded. The rope was being let down by a Win Peg and it was nearly down when somebody in the crowd raised an alarm which caused the men to let go the peg. The arms of the peg when loose caused a Whistling Sound in the air and this caused a sudden and most terrible panic among the crowd who tried to run in all directions. But the night was very dark but on they went in all directions making for anywhere until they fell by scores into the holes which like traps were awaiting them. The groans and cries that night were past description. Some were cut and bruised and cut quite badly. Some I saw whose shins were peeled from garter to boot. Some had lost their hats and one had a shoulder put out and another had his arm broken. The scene was a painfull one yet in some respects it was as ludicrous as it was painfull. Preaphs the most wonderfull thing is that after all two men were got out alive from the pit.

It has been my unffortunate lot to see more of the destructive results of Colliery Explosions since then for since that day they seem to have gone the round of the District and have occurred at some very unexpected places and for the information of those who are happily ignorant of what takes place during an explosion I will give you a description of one. The Day of the Lord cometh as a theif in the night in the which the Heavens will pass away with a great noise and the Ellements shall melt with a fervent heat.

In a firey Seam makeing Carbureted Hydrogen an Explosion may be brought by many known causes and probably from some causes that are at present unknown. Inadequate ventilation, a slight derrangement in the ventilation from an open door broken air stopping, a fallen Brattice, a slack furnace or fan, a fall of roof in the air way, an outburst or Blower, a change in the atmosphere, a fast or a Blown out shot, a Gob Fire, broken lamp, lucifer match and many other causes. In the best managed firey mine events may take place that will give conditions most favourable to an explosion in the course of a very few hours and in some cases in a very few minutes. The carelessness of a man or the forgetfulness of a boy may and often does endanger the lives of every man in the pit, and of all the calamities that afflict our race there is none more destructive or that offers less chance of escape.

Let us assume that from some of the above causes the gas in a District fires. In the mine are hundreds of men and boys cheerfull as birds and as merry as crickets. It is followed by a loud report — more prolonged than an ordinary shot. The air vibrates and seems to lift the heart out of its place it is followed by a Wild Hurricane of Red hot Dust and Blue and Yellow flames. It goes past as on the wings of lightening. Pockets or bags of Gas are drawn from the Goafs and out of the way places and even out of the solid to feed the firey tide. Men and material are carried before its rage like chaff. Men, ponies, boys, wagons, timbers are thrown together in the most

'A Reminiscence of a Collier's Life'

horrifying heaps. The fire storm sweeps down timbers, stoppings and doors in its deadly march and with these blockades all ways of escape if it were otherwise possible.

The scene that a few minutes ago was full of Life and Joy and Song is now all silent except for the cracking of burning timber or falling roof and by the glare of the burning Brattice dimly visible through the smoke are the now unrecognisble forms of Brothers and Fathers and Sons prostrate in death.

We must go now to another District out of the reach of the actual fire and see what takes place there. Suddenly they are startled by a sound as of distant thunder followed by a gust of wind that sweeps open every door and blows out nearly all the lights. The ponies on the horse roads commence to winnow and on every landing the boys and the men shout "What's That!" and one of the fire men runs out to the top landing and shouts to the men, "Look out men! She's fired somewhere. Make the best of your way to the pit and take the lads with you. Don't stop for your clothes." While he is shouting in comes the hot air and he percieves the ventilation is going the wrong way and he smells the deadly Afterdamp coming in. His men have gone hurrying past down the dips only one in a dozen haveing a light. He himself is left in the dark. But we will take it he is an old well experienced man and he knows his way to the shaft in the dark. He tears a piece from his shirt and ties it around his mouth and over his nose only just so he can breath through it. Dropping on his knees he prays, "God help me this once," and he hopes to take the men and boys before him out to the pit. He stumbles his way down the dips but finds the air now hot and almost at a stand. The afterdamp becomes more strong. He knows full well now how much will depend on a determined will and clear brain. So keeping his head down and his mouth well covered he presses on. At the bottom of the dips he is horror struck by tumbling on the body of a dead pony. He feels around for the boy but the wagons are upset and the poor lad lies under them. The poisonous afterdamp is now so strong upon him that he has not a moment to lose. He struggles determinedly on over falls and over the bodies of his comrades who have been overcome and are just sleeping the last spark of life out. For a moment he falls and his legs lose their strength, a singing noise is in his ears and it is with a desperate struggle he tries to crawl and with his face downward he feels relief and in a few yards his legs feel stronger and again he is able to walk, half faint and giddy but still determined. He fancies the air is a little more pure. Still he continues to pass prostrate forms to whom he can offer no help. The moaning of a lad startles him and pity overcomes him and groping for the lad he finds him and, happy for him, he is still conscious and in a moment he buckles his strap round the lads arm and tells him "Come along", and he tries to pull him forward. He finds the lad stumbles every yard and time is precious, and he puts the strap around the lad and drags him on by mean force. He fancies he can just see a light in the distance but his head swims, he cries in despair, "Help," and stumbles forward prostrate. He hears, He feels, He sees nothing. But he is saved and he has saved the lad. Strong arms of the explorers are around him and he is carried to the surface and the boy with him and the news fly to his cottage that the dead is alive again.

'A Reminiscence of a Collier's Life'

The explorers are bands of heroic men who go down to the rescue immediately "She has fired," They're a sort of Life Boat Crew who take a dive into a sea of fire mingled with the most poisonous of gasses. They are prompted only by a humane hope that comrades below are awaiting their coming as their only chance of life. Once down — what awful sights they see. They crawl by the dead in search of the living under tons of broken roof over falls that choke the ways between heaps of broken wagons under immense bags of gas. The firey dust blisters their hands and scorches their knees, the afterdamp makes their eyes run their heads begin to swim the recollection of their whereabouts is gone. They fancy they are home again and do not feel the arms of death that are tightening their grip around The rescuers must be rescued and well is if one or two of the party have strength to do it. If not, they sleep by the men by the side of their brothers they came to save. The paltry medals of earth, if bestrid with flashing diamonds cannot be-speak the heroism of a single hour spent by an Exploring Band.

When the Hartley Beam broke there was a cage full of men coming up the shaft and there did not seem to be the least chance for one of them to be alive. Tons of metal, tons of material went down followed by a downpour of water. When all was still, the Banksman heard a voice down that awful shaft singing,

> "On Jordan's stormy banks I stand
> And cast a wistful eye
> To Canaan's fair and happy land

'A Reminiscence of a Collier's Life'

Where my possessions lie."
The Banksman called down, "Who's there?" And a voice replied,
"It's Billy Watson."

Having graduated at Kidsgrove from Door Boy to Collier I worked Bunkers Hill for about 12 months as loader 6 months of this time work was scarce and wages low. I loaded over 60 loads for 3 shillings and four pence per day. In the summer months I earned a little under 10 shillings a week, paid 2/7 per week rent and lived as best I could on the rest. I worked three days a week on meal porridge and played three days on what they called "soakies'. I worked for 6 weeks with a clog on one foot and a shoe on the other. Because I had determined by the help of my wife I would never go in debt.

Do you see I had then married a wife to help me. To help me with a kind word when I could not get one elsewhere, to help me in every honourable resolve and righteous purpose. To help me by making my few daily wants her constant study. To help me with smile when the days were dark, and she was one of the daughters who could prophecy saying, "There's a good time a' coming lad. Wait a little longer."

I worked for some time at Slappenfield as collier, then as pit sinker. I was one of the constructers for sinking from the 7 feet to the 8 feet seam. I was then contractor for the crut to the Talk Hurst pit. I then was collier again. The pit made large quantities of gas, the ventilation was very irregular, men fired their own shots and worked with unlocked lamps. Before the

'A Reminiscence of a Collier's Life'

crut of the Talkhurst pit was Thurled I had an adventure I have not yet forgot.

One very cold frosty night I left my work to come up and I found the down cast cage at the bottom. It was a Brattice pit, split in two halfs and on each side there was very spare room for the cage to travel. Old Joe Hackney said, "You put your arm straight down by your side. Keep your elbows well in and slip down." Well it so happened that I had slipped down but I could not slip up again. The Frost had blocked my way out, for when I came within about 30 yards from the top the Engine stopped. The cage had cut itself fast in the ice. Tom the engine chap came to the top to ask me what he must do. He said he should break the rope if he went any further.

I was in the dark, I told him to let me down again I should freeze to death there. He went to his Engine I heard the slack rope rattle on the top of the cage I squat on the bottom of the cage expecting to go away with a drop too much, but it stuck fast. When he found out the cage was not going he came to the top in great alarm and wanted to know what he must do next. And that was just what I wanted to know. The cage whould not go up or down and I was freezing. I said you must pull me up somehow. What if I break the rope said he. "Go on" I shouted and he did go on and jerk after jerk I was landed.

I stood on the bank early one morning and saw the same man run 8 men in the pulley but none of them were hurt.

'A Reminiscence of a Collier's Life'

Working one night with only one other mate, he in a top heading and I in a lower one I found I could not keep my lamp cool. I went into his place and told him I thought the air bad and I asked him if he whould go out. He said no it was no worse than last night so we worked hard to get our shift done and about one o'clock I heard him punching. I was just finishing cutting my bottom and when I crawled over the heap of slack behind me to fetch my punching tools I heard him charging. I was so rucked up with stuff I could only just crawl over. At half past one he fired, not only his shot but some thing else. I saw the levil full of fire which came in a red and blue cloud to my heap of stuff but did not come over it. I lay for a minute flat in my cutting and then as all was dark I crawled over the slack to go in search of my mate. I went to the first thurling and shouted but he did not reply. I went to the next thurling and shouted his name he did not reply but I heard the poor chap groan. He had taken the precaution to go a long way back from his shot but it had caught him. I got him home as best I could but no enquiry was made about it.

I took a strong dislike to the state of things there and on the Friday I obtained my liberty from Mr Oswald. I made up my mind I should try to get my living without the pick and after working hard and getting very little on Friday night. I took my picks home on Saturday morning after breakfast that morning, I wrote (in imitation of Mark Japper?) the following lines.

Shall it be with a tear or a smile — Old Pick
That I bid thee farewell for a while — Old Pick
Shall thou and I part with a pang at the Heart

'A Reminiscence of a Collier's Life'

Or in cold hearted stoical style — Old Pick

In truth it must be with a tear—Old Pick
For much that is near and dear — Old Pick
The lingering mind looks sadly behind
In doubt and reluctance and fear — Old Pick

Yet ever by land or by sea — Old Pick
God helps us where we be — Old Pick
My babes he will keep awake or asleep
And happily travel with me — Old Pick

And thus with a spirit of rest — Old Pick
I'll trust him for what he sees best — Old Pick
With a hearty goodwill my work I'll fulfill
And do what I do — for the best — Old Pick

To the world I'll turn my face — Old Pick
Seek bread in a wider space — Old Pick
Wherever I roam I'll there make a home
Make Brothers in every place — Old Pick

And if I should need thee again — Old Pick
We never a word will complain — Old Pick
Together we'll stand. With thee in my hand
We'll labour with might and main — Old Pick

I intended to forsake coal mining for ever. That afternoon I got a note from a Colliery Master to come to his office. I went on the Monday and was engaged as Deputy. The seam was very fiery and a' many had been burned — one had died.

'A Reminiscence of a Collier's Life'

This was at the Talk-o'-th'-Hill Colliery and 10 weeks prior to the great explosion I was appointed Deputy in the pit that had 'fired'. My Overman was the Brother in Law to the Manager. He was totaly unfit for the office. There were at this time 8 Deputies under him besides myself 9. I was very unhappy and such was the state of things I gave in my notice 3
weeks before the explosion but I was persuaded to stop on again. The job was hatefull to me. The pit was making large quantites of gas — no rules were enforced — and if a Deputy complained about the gas he was told to get out more coals.

We were working night and day and there was a contest which could get out the largest quantity and every man and boy was excited over it. And Ed Dutton and I were daily reminded by our Superiors that we must devote our whole attention to it. And he in the day shift, I in the night our work was to get out coals. Every man Boy and Horse worked under one only law, the place knew no other "Get out more Coals"

The Mines Regulation Act was not in force. It did not come into operation for 6 years afterwards and I am describing the state of more than Talke Colliery when I say that discipline was not enforced. The general system of ventilation was bad and inefficient. Firemen were little better than pit labourers and were allowed no controls of the men. Shots were fired by any body any how. Brattice was not put up until gas was too strong to brush out with a jacket. In some places men unlocked their lamps and worked with naked lights.

'A Reminiscence of a Collier's Life'

Men ask in alarm now, "Why on earth did men venture into such a pit" — My answer is that men had not the Experience of explosions they have now and no one expected so sudden so great a calamity.

But the 13th of Decr 1866 came, never to be forgotten while memory lasts.

I left the pit that morning at half past 3 and met Sam Kennyon the day fireman going in and bid him good morning for the last time. At 5 o'clock he returns and tells his chief he has found all right. Dutton takes his place in the powder magazine to give out the powder (this was at the 7 feet lift near the top of the drop pit which was afterwards sunk). At 6 o'clock all are started for another days work and the same push and energy is displayed. At 11 o'clock all has gone well and there is the prospect of the biggest day's output on record. Fletcher the Overman has nearly completed his rounds and is returning from the Middle level District to his Breakfast. He has just come down the top dip. Dutton is at the bottom of the dips at the top of the crut leading from the pit bottom, loads are getting slack and he has sent the Road man to sharpen the lads up. He has " wrapt on" at the dip and away goes The Journey. In this dip just below the meeting is a curb and on this curb is an air door built in with brattice only and this is the only means of sending air into the far end workings. A Boy sits in a hole and pulls the door open with a string while the journey goes through. This was always a dangerous spot as the wagons coming quick round the curve whould tip over and did so frequently. Dutton listens for the full ones 7 in number to pass this curve but over they go one on top of the other right in the door way and he hastens up to them and calls for the road man from the top end to come and in the return heading he is awaiting help. — We will leave him there a moment and see what is going on in the New 7 feet. — All is busy and gay and cheerfull four men on one of the landings have just done their work. They are Wage men and came in early this morning to put on a landing and now they are ready when they have their jackets to go home. Let us go to the far end workings and see what is going on there. They are waiting for emptys for their loads can not pass until the journey is right in the dip. We get to the bottom of the dip and find the air is not in circulation for the door is open on the dip and the loads are very badly of the road and the whole place smells very warm.

In the heading we see 3 men at work and one of them has a naked light. His lamp top is 6 yards back on his jacket. A thirling is started down hill and a man is there punching a hole. His lamp top is off. Let us see what these other men are doing up the dip. The loader sits behind his wagon, he has been waiting ten minutes. He has a big heap of stuff down and one of the colliers says to the other, "Smoke" which is a signal for rest. They stop working. One of them takes out his pipe and lights it with a match. "**She Fires**." — a loud report — and with a terrific rush the fiery blast goes forth on its murderous errand. One of the men in the bottom head runs for the dip and the blast returning from the level picks him of his feet and hurls him against the rib and his skull is broke. All there perish instantly.

'A Reminiscence of a Collier's Life'

We left Dutton in the return air way end where he receives the full force of the fire. It rushes over him and carries everything moveable along with it. The 7 empties standing in the dip 50 yards from the top are carried up before it and split to match wood. A Blacksmith 3 minutes ago left the bank in is just come through the doors at the lift and he meets the full forces of this flying storm and is so mangled as to be unrecognisable.

Strange that any should have been got out alive from this spot yet two live but were fearfully burned. The storm must at this point turn an acute angle and its mad fury may thereby be abated. But No! Close to is the Powder Magazine and again the vengeance of fire is awfull. It flies forward to the next landing where is Fletcher and a number of boys and they fall in heaps before it. Now the flames die away but the blast of wind and hot dust goes everywhere. In the far workings a consultation is held and some propose going out the lower way and they live. Others prefer going out the usual way and they fight death for one hundred, two hundred yards and then embracing each other they lie down to die.

We will again see what of the men in the new 7 feet. We left four that had just finished work. Their names were Knowles, Jenkinsons and Yoxall. They collect their tools and are starting when the loud distant thunder peal is heard. Tom Knowles says, "Good God chaps what is it?' Will Jenkinson replies, "It is a death summons for many and is preaphs for us." When in comes the rush of wind and below them they can hear the men and boys running and shouting and the air is now

'A Reminiscence of a Collier's Life'

going the wrong way. "Stop a bit," says Yoxall and dropping on the plates on his knees he prays for his wife and his children by name. The Jenkinsons do the same and looking in each others faces they say solemly, "Not my will O Heavenly Father but Thy will be done," to which each responds Amen. It was only a short run from there into the arms of death. Two of them ran back into the workings where we found them alive.

On re-opening the colliery I was appointed the Underviewer. We had lost 91 men and 36 horses all my colleagues as deputies were dead with the exception of two. It took us 5 days and nights to bring out the dead in some cases we took the coffins in the mine to men. The manager fell ill and the work of rescue was laid upon me. We got out 45 alive. Some died of their wounds afterwards. In doing this we had to face death on all sides. Many of my comrades fell senseless at my feet and were as often as they fell carried out by others. At one time a large body of gas was met coming down a dip right upon some bags of burning corn. I called out to my men to run for their lives. They did so and got safe to bank all of them. I ran into the gas and struck down a brattice cloth that we had put up and so turned the gas another way only a moment more and it would have been on the fire. In doing this I had put out my light and before I could get back to the air I fell and lost all consciousness. I must have lain there for some time until the men on the bank finding that I did not knock for the cage concluded that I was lost, and the news was sent to my home that I was dead. Every moment the pit was expected to fire again and the crowd was cleared back to be out of danger. She did not fire. I had turned the body of gas another way. Luke

'A Reminiscence of a Collier's Life'

Foster and John Birch at length volunteered to fetch me up. I was brought to bank and laid out on some timber and the doctors brought me round.

The men who had seen the gas and the stables on fire wisely refused to go back. In the course of an hour I was ready again. My head was fearfull, my eyes were bloodshot and I trembled in every limb with weakness. But the mothers and wives and sisters with broken hearted suspense waiting for their loved ones, dead or alive as the case may be.

During this time the manager did not appear on the scene. I took John Birch aside and I said, "Don't you think we can put it out John?" He said he was afraid not. I took two buckets of water and a wet cloth and went down alone. He promised to follow if I did not come up again. I did not go up again but got to the fire and spread my wet cloth over it in the which I was burned in several places but I put out the flame and kept them down till to my joy I heard the voices of three men who had come after me. I called them forward and in 10 minutes we had put out the fire and saved the pit and several were got out alive after.

We drew back to get a bit of fresh air when I heard someone call my name. Starting to my feet I called back. It was Charley Dutton fast behind some broken wagons. We made a rush to go through a column of Black smoke and afterdamp but had to fall back. While making this attempt Mr. Wynn the Inspector came and made a brave effort to get at the lad but failed to get so far as we had been before he fell and had to be carried out of the pit and meantime poor Charley died only a few yards in front of us.

I cannot find time to give you the detail account of what followed. For 5 days and 4 nights without rest or sleep I led exploring bands fighting death inch by inch carrying out the poor fellows as best we could. Sometimes we rolled them up in brattice cloth and at other time got them on our shoulders or backs until the smell whould overcome us and we fell the living and the dead together. A little brandy was at these times found usefull but I took instead of brandy an occasional cup of Cammomile Tea, and while my staff relieved each other every four hours I remained and never left my post. Before all the bodies were out we had to take their coffins into the workings. They were unfit to be seen. But they were all brought out. The roads and plant a complete wreck. Every wagon was broken up, all the stoppings and doors were blown away.

You ask a Manager of a fiery mine if he knows of any real near escapes and he will pull out his pocket book and tell you if he thinks fit of a score that he knows about and what of the many he knows nothing of. I might give you a score I will give you two only.

One occurred during the time I was Overman, one of my districts were of work and I sent a man and a boy to fetch a train load of rails out of it. They did so. This district was making gas freely but we had plenty of air and there was seldom any seen. I saw the man when he came to his breakfast

'A Reminiscence of a Collier's Life'

and he sid, "Mister I made a blunder when I were fetching those rails out" "What with," I said. "I propped the bottom doors open and I forgot to shut them again. But I shut them as I came down." This was in the cabin at the pit bottom and I saw at once that the ventilation had been cut off for four hours in which time those workings whould fill full as an egg and that he had turned the full current on this body of gas and at that very moment it whould be coming down to the furnace which was then in the return airway. I sprang to my feet and almost screamed at him, "Follow me." I took a pick and ran along the levil to the first stopping and broke it down I then ran up the return air way where I met the gas coming in a Body but I was in time to keep it back or not one of us should again have seen the light and it whould have been impossible for any one to have told how it had happened.

Another instance was one that happened when I was Underviewer. In one District we had 3/4 of an acre of Goaf standing open on the rise of where the men were working.

This great cavity was kept ventilated up to its highest point. A ridge of dirt was built forming a wall up the middle and a brattice door at the bottom and was left open where the men were working to travel through. This place was as a rule traveled by the fireman before lighting any shots but not having found any gas for months he was content to fire a shot one day without going his rounds. It was in what is known as Bucks End District. I was nearing the top of the dip when I heard a shot and I met the fireman on the landing. I asked him my usual questions as to his district which he answered very satisfactorily. We then walked together up to the men and looked round. I then started to round the Goaf as usual when just past where he had fired his shot my lamp was put out with gas. I drew carefully back and seeing that none of the men had noticed my lamp I wispered to the fireman to take all these men down the dip before him and tell them to go up and keeping my position between the gas and the men I kept them from danger. The fireman returned in a mystery when he had sent of the men to know why? He saw my face as pale as death and asked, "What's up" I shewed him what he had done. He had actually fired a shot close upon 3/4 of an acre of gas. He trembled in every limb. We returned down the dip to consider matters when I saw my Chief comeing up. In a great passion he began to comment on my conduct in sending out the men. I told him when his temper was cooled down I whould explain. He saw by my looks there was something serious. I then took him and shewed what I had seen. But it makes one sick to think what may happen. I mention these cases to shew how great the responsibility of every man who works in a fiery mine.

Just over 6 years after the first explosion there followed another one in another seam in the same pit. It came on us very unexpected. The ventilation was good and inspections were constantly made by the most scientific mineing Engineers. My Chiefs were two gentlemen who could be unsurpassed for skill in working fiery mines. Law was respected by every man and boy in the mine, every breach of rule was punished without mercy. But she fired. I came up the pit about 12 to return again about 1 to find about 19 poor fellows gone into Eternity. Again began the horrid work I have

'A Reminiscence of a Collier's Life'

tried to picture before. Some of the poor men who escaped the first fell in this. The cause was for a good while a mystery until Proffessor Abel found by experiment that the dust was nearly as explosive as powder. This was much discredited although it came from so high an authority but since then I have known a man badly burned in the open air by the same dust thrown on the boiler fires with a shovel.

I have read a paper on the subject before the Institute of Mineing and Mechanical Engineers which was ordered to be printed for their use. I have assisted at several colliery explosions since then for theirs is scarcely a fiery pit in the neighbourhood but has had its explosion. In most of them the inspector sent me a telegram to meet him there but he often found me down there when he came.

I have been in the front of many great emergencies and I have had the honour of being trusted with the most hazardous undertakings in the most dangerous mines in England. I have won the confidence of a large number of mining gentlemen and was made a member of the Counsel of the North Stafford Institute of Mining and Mechanical Engineers. I met my inspectors with the greatest of pleasure and joined them in making mineing experiments. I shall always feel a pleasure in their company.

I am in Derbyshire because I am sick and tired of fiery mines and my memory stand charged with scenes and incidents in mineing life which whould take some days to tell. I have found in times of great peril a firm trust in the living God that has

'A Reminiscence of a Collier's Life'

never for a moment forsaken me and among colliers I have seen deeds of heroism that whould have received Royal Acknowledgement but for the jealousy of their officers who whould not let their names be known but to every collier in the land I should like to say,

"Stand up Erect! Thou art the form and likeness of thy God.
A soul as dauntless mid the storm of daily life. A heart as pure as breast ere bore.
What then! Thou art as fine a man as moves. As moves the human mass among.
As much a part of the great plan with which creations dawn began as any in the throng. Who is thine enemy?
The high in station — or in wealth thy cheif?
The great — who cooly pass thee by — with proud steps — and averted eye.
NAY, nurse not such beleif.
If true unto thyself thou wast! What were the proud ones scorn to thee.
A feather! which thou mightest cast aside — as idley as the blast. The light, the light leaf from the tree.
NO — uncurbed passion. Low desire — absence of noble self-respect — Death in the breasts consuming fires to that high nature that aspires for ever. Till thus checked these are thine enemies — Thy worst. These chain thee to thy lowly lot — Thy labour and thy life accursed.

'A Reminiscence of a Collier's Life'

O Stand Erect! and from them burst and longer
suffer not Thou art thyself thine enemy.
The Great what are they better — as theirs — is
not thy will as free? Has God with equal favours
thee neglected to endow. — True — wealth thou ast
not 'Tis but dust, Nor place, uncertain as the wind —
Thou has that with thy daily crust and water.
Mayest despise the lust of both. A noble mind! and
passions under ban. True Faith and Trust in God.
Thou art the peer of any man! Look up then! That
thy little span of life be nobley trod."

CHAPTER FOUR

STAFFORDSHIRE SENTINEL, SATURDAY 15TH DEC 1866

DREADFUL COLLIERY EXPLOSION AT TALK-O'-TH'-HILL

EIGHTY SEVEN PERSONS KILLED

FIFTY EIGHT DEAD BODIES RECOVERED

On Thursday, at Talk-o'-th'-Hill, occurred one of those fearful events which occasionally are permitted, as though for the express purpose of alarming the timid, awaking the torpid, warning the dissolute and impressing on all the lesson, "In the midst of life we are in death." At one moment a large industrial community were actively engaged in their usual avocation; the next, but few of that community were left to tell the tale of the dread calamity that had overtaken them. Truly it is declared in Holy Writ of human life, "In the morning it groweth up and flourisheth, in the evening it is cut down and withered." On Thursday, eighty seven men and boys left their homes, hearty and without thought of danger and wives and children or mothers and sisters anticipated the hour of their return but when next looked upon,

"Behold, they were all dead corpses."

THE EXPLOSION

The dire calamity which we have thus briefly introduced is, we are assured, without parallel in Staffordshire in respect of the sacrifice of human life, and is the more to be deplored because every possible precaution has been taken by those in authority to avert any, even the slightest, casualty. The scene of the dreadful event is Talke Collieries, near Talk-o'-th'-Hill – a village, as probably most of our readers know, situated about four miles from Newcastle, three from Tunstall and a mile and a half from Kidsgrove. Ten years ago a company was formed, under the Joint Stock Companies Act, for working the rich coal and iron mines in this neighbourhood, and was styled The North Staffordshire Coal and Iron Company. During that period the works have been gradually extending until, at the present time, the company not only carry on very extensive mining operations in the neighbourhood of Talk-o'-th'-Hill, but have erected two blast furnaces near their collieries. About eighteen

IN
MEMORY
OF

GEORGE JOHNSON,
LATE MANAGER OF THE
NORTH STAFFORDSHIRE COAL AND
IRON COMPANY, LIMITED;
TALK O'TH HILL,
WHO DIED THE 12TH DAY OF JANY. 1868,
AGED 46 YEARS,
AND WAS INTERRED IN THE CEMETARY
ADJOINING THIS CHURCH.

"THIS TABLET WAS ERECTED BY SOME
OF HIS SORROWING FRIENDS, AND THE
WORKMEN OF THE ABOVE COMPANY;
AS A HUMBLE TRIBUTE OF THE
UNIVERSAL RESPECT HE HAD GAINED
DURING HIS RESIDENCE IN THIS PARISH,
BY HIS UNCEASING EFFORTS TO PROMOTE
THE WELFARE OF ALL."

Memorial tablet Talke church – George Johnson

months ago, a new seam of coal, called the Banbury seam was discovered, and up to the present time the mine has been very successfully worked, there being a shaft 350 yards deep with an up and a down cast. There are two dips, one called the 'seven foot' commencing at the bottom of the shaft, and the other, termed the 'eight foot', sixty yards higher up. Early on Thursday morning 180 men and boys went to work down this pit, the No 1 Banbury, and also down an adjoining mine with a shaft 300 yards deep, known as the 'Number 2, 10 foot, there being a communication between the two pits. Everything was in perfect order, there was not a naked light in the pit, and every precaution was taken by means of bratticing, &c. to conduct the foul air – which, it appears, was exceedingly strong in connection with this particular seam of coal – to its proper place of exit, or confine it to those parts of the mine where it would be less dangerous. In fact it was well known that the pit was particularly dangerous, and every possible step was taken, which science or ingenuity could suggest, to prevent an explosion. The men knew this and were inspired with confidence to follow their perilous

calling in an unusually dangerous mine. But a very slight accident such as the breaking of a lamp or an act of carelessness very trifling in itself, such as the unscrewing of a lamp to remedy some little defect, was sufficient to send the dreadful messenger of death into every nook and corner of the mine. Something of this sort must have taken place on Thursday morning, for at a quarter past eleven, an hour before the time when the greater proportion of the men would have left the mine, a fearful explosion took place. The noise at the surface was somewhat subdued though heard at a long distance, but the miners and others on the pit banks knew too well what had happened when they saw a cloud of smoke and dust rush from the shaft of the No. 1 Banbury, and when they perceived that the cage attached to the down cast had become detached from the rope and fallen to the bottom of the shaft.

AFTER THE EXPLOSION

The greatest consternation prevailed over the village of Talke and the numerous groups of houses scattered over the surrounding districts, and hundreds of men, women and children, screaming and shouting

71

Headstone – John Samuel Kenyon

came rushing to the mouth of the pit. Mr. Johnson, the manager, and Mr. Nichols, the underlooker, immediately placed themselves at the head of a body of men who volunteered their services in rescuing the unfortunate men from their awful position in the pit. A number of men are said to have made their way from the pit, when the explosion took place into the No. 2 mine, but such was the confusion at the time that no account was taken of their numbers. We were informed by one person that between forty and fifty thus made their escape. But the attention of the rescuing party was directed mainly to the shaft of the No. 1 pit, and in the course of half an hour a number, some dead and others alive were brought to the surface. The hooker-on at the bottom of the shaft was found to be blown to pieces. The agonised cries of the many women and daughters of the unfortunate men at the pit mouth now increased in intensity – some rushed about in despair, screaming in a fearful manner, while others stared as if stupefied at the excitement of those around them. So fearful had these demonstrations become, that it was found necessary, for the sake of preserving the equanimity

of those forming the rescuing party, to order all the females from the neighbourhood of the colliery, many of them being induced to go to their homes, there to await information of the fate of their relatives. In a short time some half dozen surgeons arrived, including Mr. Greatorex, Mr. Bentley, Mr. Bruce of Kidsgrove and Mr. Salt of Audley. Dr. Barnes, of Newcastle, was also present for some time. All these gentlemen were indefatigable in their attentions to the few men who were brought up alive. The latter, most of them severely injured, were carried into the cabin, and treated by the surgeons as each particular case required. Mr. Johnson, the manager received very valuable assistance from Mr. Homer, manager of the Chatterley Collieries, Mr. Addy, manager at the High Carr Collieries and Mr. Cox, manager for Mr. Robert Heath.

NIGHT SCENE AT THE PIT MOUTH

During the afternoon Mr. Wynne, the Government Inspector of mines went down the pit, and remained there for some time. The ventilation arrangements were, of course, utterly disarranged, and the work of recovering the dead bodies became more and more dangerous, until, shortly after eight o' clock, the gas became so strong at the pit mouth, that all fires were ordered to be put out, and there was nothing to light the workers at the top of the shaft but a few safety lamps. The scene here, when darkness set in, was most shocking. A cart was waiting to receive the dead bodies. In the cabin were a number of miners whose faces were dimly lighted up by their safety lamps. They were waiting to take a turn at the work of rescue and those who had already assisted in this way were telling in low, melancholy tones the sad scenes they had witnessed – how Bill So– and – So was seen lying in such a place; how a little further on were "eight on 'em, lying all of a ruck,"; how the leg of a man had been found about forty yards from his body; how three dead horses blocked up the way to part of the works; and how one poor little boy was found dead clinging to the neck of the horse he had been riding. At intervals the cage of the up-cast shaft arrived at the surface bringing two or more dead bodies, some dreadfully mutilated, in charge of one or two of the rescuing party.

The stiff, blackened corpses, with arms rigid and outstretched, some half naked and others almost dressed, were removed from the cage by three or more men, and their faces were subjected to a short scrutiny by the aid of the safety lamps, for the purpose of identification. The cage, each time it was lowered, contained others of the rescuing party.

THE LIST OF KILLED given below, includes the fifty-three whose bodies have been recovered and identified, five whose bodies have been recovered and not identified and twenty four villagers who were known to have been in the pit when the explosion took place.

1   Edward Denby, who leaves a widow and a daughter.
2   John Grindley, single
3   John Fynney, left a widow and two children
4   Samuel Harrison, left a widow and two children
5   Enoch Smith, single
6   Matthew Sherratt, single
7   George W. Evans, left a widow and two children
8   William Robinson, single
9   Daniel Ball, left a widow and four children, and was the only support of his mother.

10 George Hicks has left a widow and four children
11 John Bosson, 13
12 William Booth, single
13 John Breeze, 13
14 James Boughey, 26 has left a widow and three children
15 Levi Cartwright left a widow and three children
16 William Washington, single
17 Samuel Johnson left a widow
18 Samuel Kennion, 35, left a widow and five children
19 Joseph Yoxall, has left a widow and three children
20 Samuel Cartlidge, 28, has left a widow and one child
21 William Stanley, 35, left one child
22 Thomas Oldfield, single
23 George Oldridge as left a widow and five children
24 Noah Billington, 30, has left a widow and two children
25 David Rigby, 14
26 Edward Dutton, 51, has left a widow and four daughters
27 Thomas Jenkinson, Butt Lane, 40 has left a widow and five children
28 William Jenkinson, 38, has left a widow and two children
29 Charles Dutton, a boy, son of Edward Dutton
30 James Rigby, 15, orphan
31 John Beddows, single
32 Thomas Griffiths, single
33 Nicholas Fletcher, 50, has left a widow and three children
34 William Ratcliffe, 40, has left a widow and four children
35 Thomas Knowles, 40, has left a widow and six children
36 James Johnson, 28, has left a widow and four children
37 Walter Fletcher, son of Nicholas Fletcher
38 Peter Twist, 15
39 John Booth, 14
40 John Yoxall, 34
41 James Sproston, 35, single
42 Henry Denby, 14
43 Samuel Benton
44 Samuel Slater
45 John Vernon
46 Thomas Berrisford
47 David Higginson, 22
48 George Kent, 19, single
49 Michael Fletcher
50 Ralph Henshall
51 Joseph Browning
52 Thomas Blackhurst
53 Thomas Daniels
54 David Colclough, 27, has left a widow and three children
55 George Reeves
56 John Hart
57 Edward Clowes, 14
58 Frederick Bailey, 22
59 George Boughey, 11
60 William Trot, 32
61 Henry Critchlow, 15

62 William Archer, 26
63 John Madder, 30
64 — Spencer, 26
65 Ephraim Cumberland, 27
66 James Thompson, 35
67 Thomas Smith, boy
68 Noah Taylor
69 Edward Smith, boy
70 John Moulton
71 Frances Brerton
72 John Macbeth
73 James Thompson
74 Daniel Cooper
75 Allan Turnock
76 Thomas Kent
77 William Cotton
78 John Murray
79 Samuel Liptrot
80 David Higgins
81 Frederick Bailey
82 George Reeves

THE CHAMBERS OF HORRORS AT THE SWAN

The fifty-eight bodies were carried, as we have said, to the Swan Inn, where two rooms had been appropriated for their reception. The bodies were divested of their outward habiliments with as little delay as possible, fourteen of them being then laid out in a room downstairs, and the remainder in the room over it. Visiting these "chambers of horrors" we found a number of colliers and relatives of colliers continually passing in and out and could not repress a thought that the inanimate contents were being made a spectacle of to a greater extent than was consistent with decency. We make this remark in perfect ignorance of the persons to blame. Whether or not there existed any official authority for the exhibition it certainly was very far from a seemly accompaniment to the scene presented to hear the constantly repeated command, "Gentlemen, please pass out, as there are more waiting to come in." It must be admitted that the deportment of the visitors was irreproachable and the ejaculations of some on recognising the lifeless corpses of those who had been their friends, showed that the lesson conveyed was not without effect. On each face seriousness was impressed; in many eyes tears glistened; by some tongues thanksgiving for deliverance was expressed. "Poor George," said one, looking on the features of George Taylor, "You have soon followed your wife," and, on inquiry, we learned that the wife had only been buried a fortnight. On one side of the upper room lay the fine robust figure of John Bossons; and near him was the equally well made Nicholas Fletcher, whose height was six feet. Fletcher, whose dead son was in the same room, was brother to the ground bailiff, and was a zealous preacher of the Primitive Methodist denomination in whose chapel at Tunstall, he preached on Sunday week. We were assured in the room, and subsequent information has confirmed the assurance, that he was a thoroughly pious man and we may here interpose the remark, that we have good reason for believing that the same remark, will apply to a large proportion of the deceased who, in this and other respects, ranked far above the average of colliers. Near a window, George Kent and David Higgins, the slight boy and the robust man, were lying feet to feet, and further on, side by side, were Edward Denby and George Reeves, the one a boy, whose body presented little appearance of injury, and the other a man whose head was shockingly disfigured, though not mutilated. Turning down one of the coverings near the centre of the room, we momentarily experienced a sickening recoil on perceiving beneath it part of a man's head. Fully half of the skull had been blown away, and the other half so slightly connected with the remainder of the head that it could be worked up and down like the lid of a box. The eyes and brains had been blown away, and a jaw bone protruded above the ghastly rim left by the carrying away of the front half of the skull. The sight was sickening, and we were glad to hide it from sight. James Boughey was much burnt about the hands, and William Cotton's face similarly injured. The skin of the boy Edward Clowes, was also much burnt. The injury sustained by Samuel Kenyon was, so far as was apparent, chiefly about the mouth, which was covered so as to partially hide the disfigurement. A second unidentified man was very much distorted. The head is completely altered in shape; the set glare upon the features tell of great horror and fearful suffering; anguish is depicted upon the countenance, and the whole picture is shocking to contemplate. Passing to almost the next still figure, that of Joseph Yoxall, we behold a decided contrast, for a placid smile still lingers about the mouth and there is an almost total absence of appearance of violence. Yoxall was a Primitive Methodist preacher, as was Fletcher, and his example, we understand, has not been without advantage to his fellow workmen. William Jenkinson, a fine looking man, was lying near him, almost unscathed to all appearance. In another place were the bodies of two youths, John Smith and Edward Smith; the latter of whom was much burnt about the face. Edward Dutton's body presented but little external sign of injury. William Smith's head was terribly burnt, but in this case there was no disfigurement. The youth John Breeze presented a peculiar appearance about the face, in which there were two large cracks looking like those sometimes seen in earthenware vessels. Peter Twist looks as though he had suffered intense agony. His upper lip protrudes at least two inches beyond the lower one, and evidently he had suffered greatly in his last moments. Thomas Murray's face and hands were very much burnt, but the countenance does not betoken suffering. The face of William Archer presents quite a marbled appearance, from the many, but not important, gashes. In the forehead is a fearful perforation, from which the blood had flowed in a stream. Close by him was lying William Robinson, and here, too, was great flow of blood from the head, the back of which had a large wound. David Rigby was much burnt about the head and four youths, slightly disfigured, were near the door. With a hasty glance at these we quitted the scene, glad to have closed our inspection.

THE INQUEST

was opened at the Swan Inn, Talk-o'-th'-Hill, yesterday, before Mr. Harding, who was assisted by Mr. Booth, his deputy. The jury was thus constituted:-

Rev. M.W.McHutchin, Talk-o'-th'-Hill
James Dickson, Clayton
Thomas Emberton, Tunstall
Henry Gillard, Tunstall
John Betley, Audley
Richard Rhead, Talk Pits
Daniel Johnson, New Road
John Turnnock, Talk Pits
John Daniels, Red Street
Thomas Sherman, Butt Lane
Henshall Moss, Red Street
Ralph Hilditch, Kidsgrove
George Shenton, Alsager
Elijah Corbett, Talk-o'-th'-Hill

After the jury had been sworn, the Coroner, addressing them, said, – "Gentlemen, – You have been somewhat hastily called together for the purpose of making an inquiry into the unfortunate occurrence which has happened in this district, such an occurrence, as I will venture to say, has not taken place in this neighbourhood since I have been coroner, and that nearly thirty seven years. Our duty today will be very short, we have simply to ascertain if these unfortunate men lost their lives by an explosion, and whether the bodies now recovered can be identified. It will be absolutely necessary to have an adjournment, therefore I mention that your duty will be merely formal, and if any other bodies be found which are not here today we can take the inquest on them at the adjournment, we would, in point of fact, be losing time if we were to go fully into the inquiry before the other bodies were recovered. I can give you no information as to the causes of the calamity; all I can mention is that an explosion has taken place and that the lives of several persons have been lost in consequence and as I before said, it would be a useless waste of time to draw your attention at present to any other points than those I have indicated. I am sorry that Mr. Wynne is not in attendance, but I do not know that your present inquiry will be materially affected by his absence, because I am not going into the point in which he will be more particularly interested as that will be done hereafter.

The jury then proceeded to view the bodies, and, on their return, the following evidence was taken;–

Isaac Boulton deposed; – I am a collier working in the middle level at the North Staffordshire Company's pit. I knew the man, Nicholas Fletcher. He was the "doggy" at the works. He was at work there yesterday morning. I saw him about half past five. I worked until about eleven o' clock before the accident happened. I do not know where Fletcher was. Where I worked I, and some other men, heard some report, from which we thought that an explosion had taken place, and we made our escape. It was the same mine (the 7 feet coal mine) that Fletcher worked in that I worked. I saw one person injured. I took him with me to the bottom of the shaft. He was able to walk. I waited for the cage to be lowered. It seemed a long time to wait. I suppose it was but a short time. I saw two boys and a man as I was coming to the shaft. They were lying dead close together. – In reply to a juryman; "I have worked there ten years." I did not stop on the pit bank after I got up, but made for home. I saw some bodies brought up. I identified Rigby and Clowes. I saw another man dead whose name I don't know. I was about four hundred yards from the pit bottom when I heard the report.

William Salmon deposed; – I live at Talk Pits. I am a collier and work at the North Staffordshire Colliery, I went to work at half past five. Fletcher had gone down when I got there. I was on the bank at a quarter past eleven, and heard an explosion from the pit. It blowed me against the hedge stakes. I saw about four men brought up. They were quite dead. Among them were the deceased James Clowes, Rigby and Smith. I am satisfied that it was the explosion which caused their death. I saw seven or eight cagefuls go down. The sound of the explosion was not very loud. The depth of the shaft was about 360 yards. I saw the two Billingtons go down. As far as I can guess there were 180 men in the pits.

William Beckett deposed; – I am a police constable at Kidsgrove and formerly at Talk-o'-th'-Hill. I have been down the works since the explosion, and many lives

have been lost. There are fifty-eight bodies lying at this house. I have examined them and I can identify thirty-four of them. The list was mulled over by the Deputy- Coroner, and the witness mentioned those he had identified.

The remainder of the fifty-eight bodies were identified by George Shenton, Schoolmaster, Primitive Methodist Schools, Talk-o'-th'-Hill, Thomas Sharman and Thomas Fryer.

During the inquest, Mr. Wynne, the Government Inspector, came into the room, covered with dirt, and said that he had explored to within twenty yards of the furthest end of the workings.

The jurymen were then bound over to appear at the adjourned inquest, to be held at eleven o' clock this (Saturday) morning, at the same place.

The work of exploring the mine in search of dead bodies was continued yesterday without intermission, Mr. Wynne, the Government Inspector, being down the mine with the exploring party during most of the day. It was stated that sixteen bodies were lying at the bottom of the shaft, ready to be sent to the surface, and that they would be brought up about midnight, and conveyed to the Swan Inn. Up to six o' clock last evening only the main passages in the mine had been explored, and it was understood that men would be working in relays all night in clearing out the various branch roads which deviate in all directions from the principal cutting. The proper amount of ventilation has been restored over that portion of the works which has been examined, a large quantity of bratticing and other materials for that purpose having been taken down the pit on Thursday evening.

Among the incidents which serve to demonstrate the general public sympathy with the sufferers may be mentioned one which reflects honour on Mr. Smith Child. That gentleman did not hear of the explosion till 9 o' clock yesterday morning, and the moment he did so he prepared to start for the scene. He had made a hunting appointment for the day, and had invited a number of his sporting friends for breakfast, but he abandoned his appointment, and, leaving his friends in his house, he started at once for Talk-o'-th'-Hill, where he placed his clear judgement at the service of the proprietors of the pit.

Other incidents include the following; – One man was working with his brother and saw him killed while he himself escaped. A boy named Samuel Colclough was brought up nearly dead at half past five on Thursday, and a galvanic battery was applied to his body for the purpose of reviving him, his moans and shrieks, while undergoing this operation were awful in the extreme, but we understand that he is likely eventually to recover. A poor widow, Mrs. Booth has lost her two sons which were her only support. One woman had lost her son, her husband and an adopted child, and has been left with four daughters. In another case there are six young children, whose mother died a few weeks ago; now the father Knowles is killed, and they are left with no-one to look after them but an aged grandmother. There are several instances in which a family of six children have been left fatherless by this dreadful occurrence. The large crowd of persons who assembled on the colliery bank and in the village, behaved well, on the whole, but there were some idle strangers whose behaviour was anything but decent. The Rev. M.W. McHutchin, incumbent of

Talk, and the Rev .Prebendary Wade, of Kidsgrove were assiduous in their attentions upon the bereaved widows and orphans. Talk, and the surrounding villages, were a sad sight to witness. The houses which death had suddenly visited were known by the blinds being drawn and, as we passed along the road, we noticed that every other house showed this sign of bereavement, and, in some instances, whole rows of six or eight bore similar evidence of the loss of some members of the family. James Withingshaw and Charles Roberts were working pretty close together in the pit some distance from where the explosion occurred. They made towards the shaft, but presently Roberts succumbed, whereupon Withingshaw said, "Come, let us rally on our hands and knees," which roused Roberts, and the two escaped. On emerging from the pit, Withingshaw sat down on the bank, exhausted, and there he was found by his wife.

The immediate cause of the disaster it has been impossible hitherto to ascertain, and, in all probability, it will never be definitely known, but it would do no good to conceal the fact that false keys fitting the Davey lamps have been found in the pockets of several of the deceased men, and this may point to the almost proverbial recklessness of the miners for the cause. One theory, however, which has been started, is not unworthy of consideration; it is that the rain which has, of late, descended in unusual quantity has, in penetrating the earth, forced the gas into the workings to such an extent as to overcome the capability of the ordinary appliances to expel it in the usual mode.

Among the officials of the North Staffordshire Provident Association, the apprehension existed yesterday, that several of their members in the village were among the victims of the explosion, and, with a view to ascertaining definitely the extent of the claims upon the society, so that provision might be made for prompt payment, Mr. Hammersley, the secretary of the society, visited the village yesterday afternoon, the result of his enquiries being a certainty, that only one member who had assured against death – Samuel Harrison, late of Bucknall – was killed.

An appeal is intended to be made to the congregations of all the places of worship in the district for funds in aid of the widows and orphans, and a subscription list has already been opened. We only add that the Rev. M.W.McHutchin, Parsonage, Talk-o'-th'-Hill, is the proper person to whom subscriptions should be addressed; and, in conclusion, would impress on the charitable the maxim, *"Bis dat qui cito dat". ("He gives twice who gives promptly"* — *Proverb; by Bacon)*

1866 explosion, Talke Pit – a man brought up

Congleton Road/Butt Lane c. 1890

The Swan Inn, Talke 1996

CHAPTER FIVE

STAFFORDSHIRE SENTINEL, SATURDAY 22ND DEC 1866

FINDING OF TWO MORE BODIES

The communication of Mr. Johnson above referred to was to the effect that two more bodies had been found in the pit a short time ago. The bodies, he believed, were those of Evans and Ashmore. He could not say whether they had been got out of the sump or not. The bodies would be brought up to bank in the course of an hour or two; they would have to be brought along the tunnel for two hundred yards, and then they would be coffined and taken to the Swan Inn. He believed there was great doubt as to whether there were any more bodies in the pit or not, as some of the men had two names, and applications had been made for one man under two different names. At about half past two the bodies of Ashmore and Evans were drawn up to bank, after having been previously coffined. They were then conveyed, in a cart, up to the Swan Inn for identification.

INQUEST ON THE TWO BODIES.

The jury, having again assembled and been sworn proceeded to view the bodies, which were in a dreadful state. The identifying witness was John Henshall, collier, Talke, who said; "I work for the North Staffordshire Coal and Iron Company. I knew Michael Ashmore and William George Evans. I have been down in the works this morning searching. I found these bodies and recognised them as the bodies of the men named. I believe they have been suffocated. They lay on their bellies, with their arms under their heads." In reply to a juryman who asked why the bodies were not found before that morning, the witness said they dared not go into that part of the pit before on account of the state of the ventilation. The coroner suggested that the inquiry should be adjourned *sine dei,* and, if any fresh bodies were found, the jury could be communicated with by the police in order that they might hear evidence of identification. This was agreed to, the coroner remarking that it was a case in which the country would require the strictest and fullest investigation, and no doubt the jury would do their best to satisfy that requirement. The inquiry was then generally adjourned, it being understood that the full inquiry would not be taken till after Christmas.

SUBSCRIPTION FROM HER MAJESTY THE QUEEN

Mr. Smith Child on Wednesday morning received the following letter from Sir Thomas M. Biddulph.

Buckingham Palace, December 17th 1866.

Sir, – Having received the Queen's command to make inquiry as to whether a subscription was about to be raised for the benefit of the relatives of the unfortunate men who have lost their lives by the colliery explosion at Talk-o'-th'-Hill and having read in the Times of today that you have opened a subscription list, I take the liberty of addressing you to request that you will put down her Majesty's name for the sum of £100 and you will signify the Queen's deep sympathy for those who have been bereaved by this terrible accident, inferior only in its effects to the one which has recently been brought before Her Majesty as having occurred near Barnsley – I have the honour to be, Sir, your obedient humble servant.

Thomas M. Biddulph.

The delivery of the letter had been delayed a day in consequence of it being directed to Hanley. The letter from Her Majesty, which produced a feeling of gratitude in the district when it became known, was acknowledged the same day by Mr. Smith Child, as follows.

Stallington Hall, 19th December 1866

Sir, – I am only this morning in receipt of your note of Monday last, conveying the intimations of Her Majesty's intentions on behalf of the sufferers from the late colliery accident at Talk-o'-th'-Hill, in this county. In the name of the committee for the relief of the widows and orphans I beg most respectfully to offer most dutiful and fervent thanks to the Queen, not only for Her Majesty's generous and spontaneous liberality, but also for the sympathy she has been pleased to express on account of this sad calamity. I feel sure that Her Majesty's kindness will be most gratefully appreciated not merely by those who will receive the bounty but by all classes of her subjects. Thanking you, sir, for communicating the Queen's commands.

I have the honour to be your obedient servant. Smith Child.

Maj. Gen. Sir T. M. Biddulph, K.C.B

PUBLIC MEETING AT NEWCASTLE

On Wednesday evening a public meeting was held at the Town Hall, Newcastle, called by R. Moseley Esq. Mayor, in compliance of a requisition signed by about thirty gentlemen, to consider as to the best course to be taken in the borough in contributing to the relief fund now being raised on behalf of the families that have been plunged into suffering by the terrible colliery explosion at Talke. The chair was occupied by the Mayor, and there was a good number of gentlemen present, including S. Allen Esq., M.P. for the borough and several ministers. – The Mayor in opening the proceedings observed that, as they were aware, the object of their meeting was for the purpose of promoting the subscriptions for the aid of the widows and children of those who had lost their lives by the late colliery explosion at Talke; by which it appeared, ninety-nine lives had been lost, as a consequence there were about forty-five widows and ninety orphans left destitute. It was certainly a dreadful calamity and one which should call for special sympathy and support. (Applause.) Mr. A. Hall rose and proposed the following resolution. "That this meeting heard with the deepest sorrow and regret of the horrible colliery explosion which occurred at Talk-o'-th'-Hill on Thursday last by which nearly a hundred lives were lost." Mr. Hall said that he thought there had never been in the recollection of any present such a dire calamity in the neighbourhood. It did not require any eloquent appeal to cause the greatest sympathy to be felt and support extended to those who had been bereaved by the explosion at Talke, – those who were wives in the morning and widows in the evening. It was heartrending and deeply to be deplored that there should be such a sacrifice of life of so many persons who descended into the earth to labour, in the pits, to contribute to the comfort of those not so employed. He felt that, under the circumstances the gentlemen present and the inhabitants of the town would subscribe liberally to the fund being raised so as, in some little measure, to secure the comfort of those individuals who had been so suddenly bereaved. (Hear, hear.) It was indeed melancholy to think that there had been so many widows made by the accident; that the support of aged mothers had been taken away, and that so many orphans were left. It was their duty to come forward and endeavour to alleviate as much as possible the sorrow which had been caused. (Applause.) – Mr. J. Lamb seconded the resolution remarking that everybody regretted the sad accident. He had often thought that if any class of men deserved good pay it was the colliers. He thought it was necessary that government should call upon colliery proprietors to provide the most effectual means for inspecting pits, and if such accidents were found to happen through a desire for economical working, that a proper inspection with a view to safety should be enforced. There had been too much laxity in these matters; men being allowed to descend the pits and smoke below, to the greater danger of themselves and others. He hoped that one result of the late explosion would be that there would be a better system of inspection introduced. The resolution was carried unanimously. Mr. W. C. Gemmell said that he had much pleasure in proposing the next resolution which was, "That this meeting records its heartfelt sympathy with the widows and families of the victims of the late explosion, and hereby resolves that a public subscription shall be forthwith opened for their relief." Mr. Gemmell observed that they all sympathised with the sufferers in their irreparable loss and the same feeling was manifested throughout the whole country. The subject had been taken up in London and other places, and doubtless large subscriptions would be raised. They could not bring back the dead to life, they could not give the bereaved the protection of a husband or father again, but they could, as far as lay in their power, alleviate their suffering – (Hear, hear) – by coming forward and responding liberally to the appeal for the charity which was called for both there and elsewhere. Mr. Gemmell then announced that Mr. B. Wickstead of Bewdley, Worcestershire, had subscribed £100, (Applause). Mr. Wickstead had given the whole of his income this year from his property in Cheshire and Staffordshire to his tenantry towards their losses by the cattle plague, so his contribution was considered to be something handsome. Sir E. M. Buller had also subscribed £50. These amounts, it was thought, could not be considered in the local contributions. The Rev. E. J. Edwards had forwarded £9 12s. 5d., amount of collections in the church on Sunday. He, (Mr. Gemmell), brought the matter before the directors of the bank with which he was connected (National Provincial Bank) and, by their direction, he presented a hundred guineas on behalf of the bank. (Applause). He doubted not but that the sum contributed would afford some consolation to the bereaved, in seeing the good feeling and expression of sympathy on their behalf. – Mr. Alderman Cartwright seconded the resolution. They all felt deeply about the matter, and it was merely a formal expression in, at the meeting, stating they felt sympathy with the sufferers by the late accident. They must, however, back that up with liberal subscriptions. He doubted not but that the contributions would be large. – The Rev. W. Chambers, Congregational Minister, spoke in support of the resolution, and remarked that without wishing to trespass upon the arrangements which might have been made as to the meeting, or without being supposed to trespass upon the generous sentiment of his fellow townsmen, he hoped that he might be allowed, as a minister residing in the town, and as one who felt a deep interest in the object that had brought them together, to say a few words in support of the resolution before the meeting. The present occasion was one which called for their deepest sympathy;

the dreadful character of the late explosion in the neighbourhood must have thrilled the whole nation. The vast number of the relatives of the unfortunate men who had perished by the awful catastrophe, who had been reduced to a destitute condition, the widows and orphans, the aged parents and helpless brothers and sisters who had been reduced to a state of destitution, should call forth the sympathy and liberality of the entire community in all parts of the country. (Hear, hear.) There was special reason why Newcastle and the towns in the district should contribute largely for the relief of the unfortunate sufferers, not only of the broad ground of humanity and of religion, but on account of their near proximity to the scene of the disaster. They were, therefore, he thought, placed under a special obligation to extend their sympathy and benevolence to the utmost of their power. (Applause.) It was little they could do to staunch the bleeding wounds that had been opened in the hearts of suffering relatives and friends, those hearts must continue to ache in solitude and grief, but what little they could do to mitigate their misery, and alleviate the pressure of their temporal distress would be cheerfully done by them all. His own congregation would, in common with other congregations in the town, make arrangements for a collection to be made on behalf of the distress fund. (Hear, hear.) Mr. Alderman H. Hall then proposed that a committee should be appointed to carry out the object of the meeting in getting subscriptions, to consist of the Mayor, the Revs. J. S. Broad, J. O. Julian, F. Hoare, J. H. Armstrong, W. Chambers, J. Terry; Messrs. J A. Hall, Lamb, H. Hall, Baildon, Hargreaves, Broomhall, Winstanley, Dickson, Harding, Cartwright, King, Mason, Litchfield, Dutton, Slaney, Williams and Umbers. He felt sure the people of Newscastle would feel great pleasure in doing the utmost in their power to promote such a good work, and his fellow townsmen would come forward, as they had on former occasions when appeals had been made on behalf of those in distress. (Hear, hear.) The accident at Talke was a most melancholy one, and one which should call for their utmost exertions to help those who had been plunged so suddenly into sorrow and distress. He felt sure the committee named would do their best in getting subscriptions to carry out the object proposed; and he would suggest that Mr. Gemmell be the treasurer. (Applause.) Mr. Alderman Dickson rose to second the resolution. He said he would not try to harrow up their feelings by describing the sad scenes at Talke, which he had witnessed, having been one of the jury that had sat upon the inquest, he could assure them that the circumstances were most heartrending. Six more dead bodies had been got out of the pit that morning, and it was the painful duty of the jury to meet together on the occasion. He was extremely pleased to see that the county and the country had taken up the question of a distress fund. Subscriptions were rolling in fast, and he was that night the bearer of a large sum of money which he had brought from Talke – (Applause) – not including Mr. Smith Child's noble subscription of £500. Not only did the gentlemen of the county sympathise in the movement, but the ladies had taken it up. Mrs. Smith Child visited Talke taking with her a considerable quantity of clothing for those who had been bereaved, and connected herself with ladies in the district to concert measures to aid the distressed. Linen and other things were provided and the expense would not come out of the general fund being raised. Mr. Dickson said that he thought the real amount of distress was not known at present and mentioned one case where the mother of seven children died a short time ago, and, on Thursday, the father was a victim of the explosion. The children were now in the charge of an aged couple from Lancashire. Mr. Dickson bore testimony to the indefatigable exertions of Rev. M. W. McHutchin and Mrs. McHutchin, and others, mentioning the name of Mr. Shenton a schoolmaster, who was almost exhausted by his hard labour. Mr. Gemmell said that the amounts he had mentioned were only those that had come into his own hands. Mr. Slaney said that when he heard that a requisition was being got up for a public meeting, he communicated with Mr. Buckley, M.P. (Conservative member for Newcastle) and Mr. Buckley had telephoned stating that his name must be put down for 10 guineas. (Applause.) Other announcements of subscriptions were made. The subscription list was then passed round the meeting. The following gentlemen subscribed five pounds and upwards; - the Mayor £10 10s., Mr. Allen, M.P. £50., Mr. Buckley, M.P. £10 10s., Mr. H. Coghill £10, Mr. J. Edwards, May Place, £10, Mr. J. A. Hall £10, Messrs. H. Hall and Sons £10 10s., Mr. J. Lamb £10, Mr. W. Hargreaves £5 5s., Mr. G. Ball £5 5s., Mr. J. Dutton £10, Mr. R. Slaney £5 5s., Mr. T. Harding £5 5sL. Umbers £5, ., Mr. W. R. Dutton £10, Mr. T. Messrs. Baker and King £10.

CHAPTER SIX

COLLIERY GUARDIAN 12 JANUARY 1867

THE COLLIERY CATASTROPHE IN NORTH STAFFORDSHIRE

The adjourned inquest on the bodies of the men killed by the recent explosion at Talke *[13/12/66]*, North Staffordshire, was held on Tuesday, at the Swan Inn, Talke, before Mr. Harding, coroner. Mr. Wynne, the government inspector of mines for North Staffordshire, and Mr. Evans, the Government inspector for the Midlands district were present. Mr. Keary, solicitor, attended for the lessees of the colliery. Several mining engineers and colliery managers were in attendance.

The coroner, addressing the jury, remarked that a good deal of anxiety was felt in the country to have the information on the subject of this catastrophe, and it was the duty of the jury to make the fullest investigation of the matter, and have to ascertain, if possible, the cause of the accident. Having asked the jury to dismiss from their minds all they had seen about the subject under inquiry in the newspapers, or had heard in any other way outside the room, and to confine their attention to, and be guided only by, the evidence they would hear that day, the coroner explained the law bearing upon the case; and, referring to the accident, observed that they ought to be thankful to have such heroic men as they had seen exerting themselves in the recovery of the dead and the rescue of the living, on the occurrence of this calamity, to the hazard of their own lives. The public must be grateful that such men were to be found; and, on the other hand, it was gratifying to know that the public had taken in hand the widows and orphans caused by the catastrophe, and had put their hands in their pockets to relieve the distress which, he was sorry to say, must exist for a long time to come. The coroner said that he had been requested by a lady from Macclesfield, who did not wish her name to be known, to hand £5 to the treasurer of the relief fund.

Mr. George Johnson, manager of the North Staffordshire Coal and Iron Company, was the first to be called. He said that he had held the office for ten years, and that the underground works were managed by Mr. Thomas Nicholls, who had been underground manager for eight years. He (witness) was in his office, between 500 and 600 yards from the pit, at the time of the explosion, and hearing a slight humming sound and seeing some smoke ascending from the shaft, he went to the bank, where he met Nicholls, who, he ascertained, had not been down the pit that morning. Witness produced plans of the workings, and, in reply to Mr. Wynne, said Nicholls was responsible for the underground workings; but they had not kept a register of the state of the pit, nor as to the air which passed through each part of the mine. Nicholls gave him a verbal report of the state of the pit on Tuesday night, but between then and the Thursday, when the explosion took place, there was no report.

Mr. Thomas Nicholls, underground manager, a miner of twenty-one years experience, said his duty was to see that the rules were properly carried out in the pit. Before the accident he had visited the workings on the Tuesday afternoon, when he found them free from gas. If anything was wrong it was the duty of the fireman to report it. He received no report that day (Thursday) on the morning of which the workings were examined by James Anderson, a man who worked in the roads, and he (witness) believed one of the firemen also examined it. If the fireman neglected his duty it was his business to report it. The men worked with lamps and they were not allowed to use candles at all. The lamps were numbered and fastened with a direct screw. It was the duty of Oldfield to give out the lamps and see they were properly oiled, cleaned and locked. It was the duty of the fireman to see to the firing of shots. The powder was used night and day as required. Witness did not believe the explosion was caused by the firing of shots. He was not aware of any smoking in the pit. Nothing of the kind had been reported to him and there was a rule against it. In the ten foot workings the 'in-take' was six feet by seven feet. In December, 18,000 cubic feet of air was passing through per minute. In the 'Two-rows' 9,000 cubic feet per minute. No complaints had been made to witness of a deficiency of air. In each mine there was a furnace. The opening into the seven foot mine was six feet by six feet six inches. The depth of the pit at that part was 300 yards.

Mr. Wynne: "Under whose direction was the pit left at the seven foot level, instead of being sunk down to a lower level?"

Witness: "I don't know who would be responsible for that. The dip of the strata was about one in four or five. Between the main level and the top of the works there would be about eight or nine places where bratticing was put up. Some time ago there was water in the dip workings, which was got out on the 11th August. Up to that time the air went out at the seven foot working. They afterwards cleared the 'jig'. The 'back-brow' was swollen in consequence of the water. It was not cleansed but a man had gone through within the last three months."

Witness was responsible for driving the bottom levels after they were stopped. He put doors on the main 'jig' to ventilate the working, and he thought it sufficient for what they were doing. Seven tubs would have at frequent intervals to pass up and down, and during that time the doors would have to be open, but that would scarcely be a second. There was another door in the main level, but there was an opening in the door to give vent to the air, which he found would not go. The air was all right when the explosion took place. The day before there was gas in the two lower levels, and they took the men away and cleared it. They had a complaint of gas some time previously when they acted in the same manner. In the bolt-holes in the north level the stoppings were brattice cloth. He did not know that smoking was going on in the pit. It had never been reported to him that any of the men had false keys. Twenty seven keys of lamps were produced. Police constable Beckett said he found these in the trousers pockets of men brought up dead out of the pit. In reply to the coroner, Beckett said he did not know where these keys had been obtained by the men, but they were common keys and might be got anywhere. Witness had never heard anything of those keys, and could not explain their being found. Fletcher, Hicks and Kenyon were allowed to have keys to lamps, and they had to fire shots. It had never come to his knowledge that anyone else had fired shots. He had never had a complaint that men had to wait an hour to fire shots; but he had heard complaints of men having to wait

Colliery Guardian 12 January 1867

some time, and they had grumbled but had never said they would not wait. They put a wire through the gauze and made it red hot, and fired with that instead of taking the top of the lamp off. Sometimes they fired with a fuse or a lighted straw. At all times there were 41,000 feet of air per minute coming out of the pit. They commenced driving the tunnel to the east on 4th November 1865, and finished it in September last. They did not sink the pit to the level of the other shaft at the same time because they at first had water and were afraid of gas. They were still sinking. There was no more water three months ago than now, so they might as easily have done it then as now. In reply to a juror witness said he could not say what was the cause of the explosion. "Someone must have had the top of his lamp off or had matches in his pocket, or something", remarked the witness vaguely. He could not say how the gas got there. There must have been a defect somewhere. They sometimes had gas from the blowers but there had always been wind sufficient to carry it away. There were a pipe filled with tobacco and three matches found near one of the dead bodies. The blowers were sudden gusts of gas, which, coming in contact with any naked light, would immediately cause an explosion. There had never been any complaint of want of air.

Charles Lawton, collier, was employed in the pit as deputy underlooker. He left the pit a little before four o'clock on the Thursday morning. He was all over the workings during the night. He noticed no indication of gas from the time he went in till the time he came out. John Henshaw, who was working at cutting in, in the lower level about seven o'clock on Wednesday evening, complained to him of gas coming from the face of the coal. Henshaw said that he told the fireman, and the matter was set right. In his opinion the works were in a safe state when he left in the morning. The men were not in the habit of smoking in his presence, but he had reason to believe that many of them did smoke occasionally; he had smelt tobacco smoke. When asked why he suspected there had been smoking, witness said it was because he knew the men were smokers. Witness had reason to believe that the men had keys and that they opened the lamps, but he

96

never found these things out. If lamps were open when he went down they were locked before he could get to them. The men knew when the underlooker was likely to turn up. (The jury complained that the answers of witness as to the smoking were not satisfactory). Witness found the pipe at the top of the up brow. The body of a man was near it. Mr. Nicholls took a match out of a coat pocket which was near. He saw Mr. Nicholls pick up a lamp-bottom against the solid coal and the top down the cutting, and that was the place where Young and Lissamore were at work. The lamp belonged to Lissamore.

A Juryman pressed the witness as to whether he had done his duty when he suspected that there had been smoking.

Witness said he had sometimes suspected, and gone to examine the place, but he never had been able to get evidence of the fact.

Jury were inclined to believe witness had known more about infringement of the rules in this matter than he was inclined to tell

John Henshaw, collier, living at Talke, said he worked at the pit in which the explosion took place on the night previous, in the bottom level. He worked there from five o'clock on Wednesday night until seven o'clock. The air was clear, and remained so until about half past six, when he sent for James Bossons, who came and examined the higher side. Bossons then ordered him to leave off work. An air sheet, which had been knocked down by the wagons, was replaced, and the gas was cleared away. He then went to work in the new seven foot seam. There was no gas there or anywhere else in the lower levels. He heard no complaints of any gas being in the pit. He had worked in the level three months and had never been stopped before. He considered that the cause of the fouling of the pit between the hours of five and seven was the drop-sheet being down. This sheet was in one of the bolt-holes between the levels. Bossons fired shots before with touch paper, which he lighted through the gauze of the lamp.

By the Jury; Witness said he never saw keys in the pit and never saw anyone smoke in the pit.

Joseph Lovatt, of New Road, said he was a collier, and was at the pit on the night previous to the explosion. He was in the bottom level above the last witness. He worked from about five o' clock up to two o' clock on Thursday morning. There was not a bit of gas in that part of the pit. There was a little gas below through the sheet being down, but it was soon got away. Witness had seen smoking in the pit, and he had not reported it – there was no smoking in his place. He should think it was a month since he had seen any smoking. He would not say it was a month before the accident. He did know that some men had keys of their lamps, and he had seen keys; he had not reported what he had seen. They fired their shots if the fireman was not there. They were obliged to do so for stuff for the loader. The firemen were in their place before and after they fired their shots, and did not say anything. They left about two o' clock and left the place safe. They fired two shots just before they left. The men who went to work in his place had worked before they were killed; one shot had been fired, and another was nearly ready. He considered himself competent as a fireman. His mate had fired shots.

John Steel, collier, Audley, stated that when he was at work in the pit on Tuesday night, the pit was clear of gas. He fired two shots; that was, the fireman did it

He used to do it when he had a gauze lamp, but when he had a glass one the fireman fired the shots. He never saw smoking in the pit, or the lamps opened. Bossons was the fireman that night. He did not send for him to fire the shots that night because he had a gauze lamp. He had heard the rules read. He had waited a long time for the fireman to fire the shots, and therefore he had fired them himself. In reply to Mr. Keary, witness said the fireman always came when he was sent for to overlook the firing of the shots.

James Bossons, fireman, stated that he worked for the North Staffordshire Company up to the time of the explosion, but he did not then. He was at work there on the night before the explosion took place. He examined all the lower workings, and they were free of gas. In about an hour after he made the examination the men began to work. His attention was called to gas on the higher side of the lower level. He stopped Henshaw from working, and found a sheet down. He put it up, and examined the various parts of the level, and after waiting for some short time, the gas was all cleared. A few shots were fired. He fired them. He could not tell how many

– about four or five. He never knew of any smoking in the pit , nor did he know of any of the men having keys of lamps. When he left at half past two or quarter to three in the morning the pit was all right. The gas would have to go through the new seven - feet. He never recollected smoking tobacco in the pit. He had no knowledge that they could not work a night without firing a shot. He did not know that Proctor and Steel fired shots on Tuesday night. He often tried the lamps in the workings, but he never found any unlocked. The men had complained about having to wait firing shots.

Daniel Heath, collier, said he was at work on the night before the explosion. He was in the heading above the lower level, which was clear of gas the whole time he was there. He heard Henshaw say there was gas in the lower level. He (witness) fired four shots during his turn on the Wednesday night. The fireman was not there but he knew that witness fired the shots, as they could not get coal without them. They got the light for the shots by touch-paper, drawing up the light from the lamp. He had never seen anyone smoking in the pit. He had never known lamps unlocked except by the fireman.

The enquiry then adjourned.

On the jury re-assembling on Wednesday morning, Mr. Wynne the Government inspector, addressing them, said he wished to remark that, at a meeting of miners' delegates, at Motherwell, on Monday night last, Mr. McDonald, who was at the head of the miners' advocates, stated; — "We have made searching inquiry, so far as our means could go, and it cost us heavy expense, into the Harecastle explosion and we find that for months and months that pit has been recognised as in a state ready to explode at any hour." — Now he (Mr. Wynne) could not state too publicly that if that had been the case he thought that those persons who had given the information were now bound to come forward and state what they knew. (Hear Hear) He had not himself the means of bringing such evidence before them; if he had he would do it, but there must be somebody who had the means of bringing that before them. They would not be doing their duty if they did not do it. This was either false or true. If it was true they ought to know all about it.

A Juror; "I should think it a deliberate falsehood, so far as the evidence has gone."

Another Juror; "Some persons should be appointed to write to the paper and contradict it."

The First Juror; "If it is true it would be better to adjourn for a few days. It will be important to have that in evidence."

The Coroner said they ought to thank Mr. Wynne for bringing the matter forward; but, inasmuch as they were engaged in a particular inquiry, it would not be well to take any steps with regard to it at present. After the inquest was over, if it should be found necessary to take any notice of it, then would be the proper time to proceed.

The examination of witnesses was then proceeded with.

James Anderson collier, employed at the pit, stated that he was at work from six o'clock on the night previous to six on the morning of the explosion, in the low level. He looked after the roads. There was no gas in the pit. Kenyon examined the lower workings and told Fletcher that all was perfectly safe at about five o'clock on Thursday morning. Hicks examined the upper workings. The ventilation of the pit always prevented an accumulation of gas.

Thomas Turnock, collier, stated that he went to work at about five o'clock on Thursday morning, when the pit was clear of gas. He saw Kenyon at the bottom. He worked in one of the middle levels and was at work when the explosion took place. It did not affect their place much; it snatched the lights, but did not snatch them out. Could not say whether any gas was fired in the upper levels.

By Mr. Wynne; He had worked in the same place a long time. The ventilation had been good. Sometimes there had been gas in that level, but not much. Twelve months back they had blowers of gas, and then they left off work. They had a little gas about a month ago in the upper level, which was brushed out with a piece of tin. There was bratticing at that level. The only blower which had caused him to cease work was in the middle level. Witness rescued a boy and got to the fresh air in about fifteen minutes.

In reply to a Juryman witness said he had seen men smoke in the pit.

Peter Hollier, banksman in the employ of the owners of the pit, said he was at work until between five and six o'clock on Thursday morning. He let Samuel Kenyon the fireman down the pit at about four o'clock and at five he let Nicholas Fletcher down. Shortly after that the workmen went down so Kenyon had been down an hour before the men went down. He heard no complaints of gas being in the pit.

By Mr. Wynne; Never heard any complaints.

By the Jury; Powder never went into the pit in barrels, half or quarter barrels.

William Salmon, banksman, said he went to work at the pit at half past five that morning. One man came out of the pit before the turn was finished. About a quarter past eleven o'clock wind and dust coming up the pit blew him against the headstock. Mr. Nicholls was shortly on the pit bank, and he and others went down in the pit. Witness, after staying for a short time went home very frightened and did not work again that week.

John Breeze, collier, was working in the pit on Wednesday night and Thursday morning, until between two and three o'clock, in the new seven foot, which was all right and free from gas. Later there was a small blower in his place but the ventilation took it off. He fired one shot in his place, getting a light from the fireman, who had examined the place. That was about one o'clock, and after the blower had lasted about a quarter of an hour. He heard the explosion, which was like a shot, and at once said, "That's an explosion." He and John Henshaw tried to go up the stable dip, but when they got about forty yards they could go no further for the damp. They saw the dead bodies of a man and a boy. They went to the pit bottom and found a number of dead. One man was brought out alive. He found a lamp unlocked. He found a pipe in the hand of one of the dead named Harrison, and a lamp key was in his pocket. Three other lamps lay near the same place but they were locked. He believed the dead he saw were not burned but suffocated.

Mr. Johnson general manager of the colliery, in reply to the Coroner, said that he had no man to give evidence who was in the upper levels. All who were there were dead.

James Withenshaw, collier, said that he was at work in the pit during the hour that the explosion took place at the top of the rise workings. The firemen Fletcher and Hicks were in the pit before he went down. His place was free from gas. There were nine colliers working close to him, five of whom came up alive. The first evidence of the explosion was a sensation of deafness when he fell down. He remained some twenty minutes afterwards; he knew there had been a fire but he did not know where it was. His light was not blown out. He went along the top levels with two others to the shaft with difficulty. They were about seven minutes on their way and passed many dead bodies.

By Mr. Wynne: They saw no fire. They waited until the damp got to them. It came along the top levels. Witness was quite clear he felt nothing to indicate a second explosion.

Charles Robert, collier, said that he went into the mine about half-past five on the morning of the explosion. He saw Kenyon at the bottom of the pit. He worked in the top level which was clear enough. Sometimes there was a little gas in it, but there was none that morning. He had not seen any for some time. When the explosion took place he felt the air draw from them. He put on his clothes and put up some sheeting

to bring up air. He waited about twenty minutes and then went with Withenshaw towards the mouth of the pit. They trod upon a number of bodies but could not tell whether they were dead or alive. They could not ascertain for they expected every minute to be their last. They had no use in their legs and arms, they were almost insensible. In reply to several of the Jury: He did not fire his own shots; he never smoked in the pit, nor had he seen anyone else do so. He had no key to unlock his lamp, and never saw any keys in the possession of the men.

Daniel Cope, collier, who worked in the pit from half-past five on the previous night until three o'clock on Thursday morning said there was no gas where he was working, and he heard no complaints of any. He was all over the place and if there had been any gas he should have seen it. Shots were fired that night by James Bossons, the fireman. The fireman gave a light to Daniel Heath. Bossons was present when the shots were fired, and if Heath said that Bossons was not sent for, and not there, he did not say that which was true.

Alfred Dale, loader, was at work in the pit at the time of the explosion, at the bottom end of the upper dip. He went to work at six o'clock and worked four or five hours. He did not notice any gas in the mine, and heard no complaints of it. When the explosion occurred he was sitting in a hole getting something to eat. He heard the noise and saw a flame pass him, which came up the main dip and along the pit level, and then up the stable dip. He never heard but one explosion. Moses Taylor, collier, said he went down the pit at about six o' clock, and worked in the new seven foot. He worked about five hours and at eleven heard the explosion. He saw Kenyon who said the pit was clear when he went down. About an hour and a half before the explosion he hit upon a blower in the stone, which was bad at first but it abated. It, however, was still blowing when the explosion took place. On perceiving the blower he sent for the fireman who put up bratticing which took off the gas. He did not fire any shots that morning.

Richard Elliott, collier, said that he worked in the new seven foot on the day of the accident. When he went down he saw Samuel Kenyon at the bottom, who said the pit was all right. Witness found his place so, and

perceived no gas until the explosion took place. He saw no blower. They had not had to complain of their places being foul. They had not been so foul as not to be able to fire their shots. Generally speaking their place were free of gas.

Henry Randels, collier, deposed; – to seeing the fireman at the bottom of the pit when he went down; – to his place of work being clear of gas; – and to the fireman always lighting his lamp and firing his shots.

James Oldfield, lamp-keeper, said he gave out all the lamps on the morning of the explosion. They were all properly locked. They were handed to him after the explosion. Lissamore's number was eighty-six. All were locked when he gave them over but some were unlocked when returned. William Booth's was unlocked, number 325. That produced was John Hart's, number 201. He never received any unlocked before.

Police constable Beckett said he examined the bodies of the deceased. He found on them twenty-seven lamp keys, about a dozen tobacco pipes, a dozen or two tobacco boxes and matches on most of them.

The inquest was then adjourned   until Tuesday next.

CHAPTER SEVEN

STAFFORDSHIRE SENTINEL, 2ND FEBRUARY 1867

TALKE COLLIERY EXPLOSION

VERDICT OF THE JURY

Yesterday the adjourned inquiry relative to the deaths of ninety -one persons in the Banbury pit of the North Staffordshire Coal and Iron Company, was resumed under Mr. Harding, coroner, assisted by Mr. Booth, deputy coroner. Mr. Wynne and Mr. Evans Government Inspectors were present, as also was Mr. Keary, who represented the owners of the pit. Mr. McDonald who had, as previously mentioned, made a statement at a meeting in Glasgow relative to the calamity, was also present, and the attendance of the general public was much larger than at any previous sitting.

The Coroner, in opening the sitting, said, – "Gentlemen, when we were here last it was determined to adjourn until today for the purpose of hearing Mr. McDonald, and also for the purpose of allowing him an opportunity for bringing any information that would bear upon the subject for your information. We have met here accordingly, and, since our last meeting, have received a letter from Mr. McDonald, requesting to know if he might be permitted to make a statement prior to bringing parties forward to verify that statement. I wrote saying that I saw no objection whatever. Under these circumstances we have met and I believe Mr. McDonald is now here. So far as I am concerned I am anxious to hear, not only from Mr. McDonald, but to receive any information I can from any person in this matter. You are here gentlemen, as I before said, to inquire into the serious and calamitous affair. Your oath is a serious one, you are sworn to inquire and true presentment make of all such matters here given you in charge, to spare no-one through fear, favour or affection and to give a true verdict according to the evidence. Gentlemen, I have the highest trust in you that you will do your duty irrespective of anything that may have appeared either before or since you last met here, and I cannot but express regret that a statement has been published and circulated about matters which, if necessary, I can verify myself, and containing statements as libelous, untrue and as false as both. (Hear,hear). For what purpose that document was round I cannot say. Can it be for the purpose of intimidating you, can it be for perverting that serious inquiry for which we are met here today. If so I am convinced, at least, that it will not succeed. I am anxious that every publicity should be given to the matter, that every information should be obtained for you, and rather than it should be otherwise I am willing to sit here today, tomorrow or a month from this time at your service, and to do that which you may direct me to do. (Hear, hear). I don't know whether it would be as well for Mr. McDonald to state what course he wishes to pursue, I am most anxious to accommodate him in every way and I am most anxious to hear all witnesses that can throw light on this shocking affair. I may add that, yesterday, late in the evening, I received a letter from Mr. McDonald requesting that certain parties should be summoned, but he must be aware that there was no time for anything of the kind. The names of three parties I received a week back were handed to Mr. Sweeting, Chief of Police, and I understand that they have received the proper intimation. This being so, the better plan, I consider, will be to ask Mr. McDonald what it is he wishes to be done."

Mr. Keary; – "I apprehend that we cannot hear Mr. McDonald unless he is sworn."

The Coroner; – "It is not evidence that he wishes to give."

Mr. Keary; – "Then we cannot receive it at all if it is not evidence. The course to pursue is to complete the evidence, and afterwards, if any person wishes to make any observations, you can decide whether you will hear him."

The Coroner; – "What I understand from Mr. McDonald's note is that he wishes to make a statement, which statement he afterwards proposes to verify by witnesses."

Mr. McDonald; – "I don't appear in this matter at all as a witness."

The Coroner to Mr. Keary; – "Do you still object?"

Mr. Keary; – "Most decidedly, I do."

Mr. McDonald; – "I have your invitation, sir to come here, and I only beg to submit this. If the legal objection on behalf of the owners of the pit is to be entertained, it would have been only fair, when the jury was last adjourned, to have said that the objection would be made, instead of having me travel from Scotland, in the face of important engagements to come here and be met in this way. But, if I am not allowed to make the statement here, I shall make it to the Home Office or elsewhere."

Mr. Keary; – "Mr. McDonald seems to say there is some want of fairness on my part, but I must remind him I never before this time heard of what he wished, or that he was to make a statement. If he wishes to give evidence, to make a statement on oath, I have not the least objection. But I have an objection to his making a statement."

The Coroner; – "On what grounds?"

Mr. Keary; – "On what I said before. I never heard of the evidence being interrupted for the purpose of allowing any person to make a statement."

Mr. McDonald; – "I come here at your invitation, sir."

The Coroner; – "Clearly so, but if there is crept into our arrangement a little irregularity, we must try and correct it. But I have not yet decided. Have you any witnesses to call, Mr. McDonald?"

Mr. Keary; – "And I reserve my objection till he calls them."

Mr. McDonald; – "I am really astonished at being met in this way. I will read the letter I have from the foreman of the jury."

The Coroner; – "I am bound to say that the objection from Mr. Keary is a very feasible one."

Mr. McDonald; – "Then I suppose you have no objection to allow me to hand the letters I have received from yourself and the foreman to the press?"

The Coroner; – "No"

Mr. McDonald; – "All right then, I shall give them to the press of the kingdom."

Mr. Emberton (a juror) strongly objected to the wasting of the time of the jury; if they were to continue as they had been doing they might go on with the inquest until Burslem Wakes. (Laughter)

Mr. McDonald asked if he might recall Mr. Coe, mining engineer of the Biddulph Company.

The Coroner assented.

Mr. Coe (recalled); – "I was not manager of Lundhill Colliery when the explosion occurred there. I was connected with the management. I left three months after."

107

Staffordshire Sentinel, 2nd February 1867

(To the Deputy Coroner) "I had been manager from the previous October. Mr. Hult became manager in January. The explosion took place in February."

(To Mr. Keary); "Mr. Woodhouse took an active part in the inquiry as to that explosion, and he recommended me to Mr. McDonald my present employer. I remember him tell I could suit myself."

Enoch Jackson, called by Mr. McDonald; "I live at Kidsgrove, and I am a collier. I have worked at the North Staffordshire Colliery. Charles Lawton came for me and engaged me. He engaged me as fireman. He also engaged my brother William. I entered upon the engagement on the 17th September 1866. My brother also was engaged as fireman. We were to work one in the night and the other in the day. Lawton, who was a deputy overman, took me into the rise workings of the seven feet. I then accompanied Lawton into the low level. I found a good deal of gas there. On the main jig I did not find any doors, but two cross sheets. I remarked to him that there ought to be two doors and two boys to mind them. He replied that they were as they would have to be. It was about one o'clock on Monday morning when I commenced and I left off about seven. I saw gas during the whole of that time. I did not go again till Tuesday evening the 18th. I went again to the low level and I found the gas increased very much. I saw that the gas was increased by the sheets being torn down in the main jig. I went to attend those sheets that night. I tried to keep them up the greater part of the night. On the first night of my engagement I saw pipes smoked. I smoked myself. I asked Charles Lawton to allow me to smoke, and he allowed me. Lawton sat by me while I did so I was close to the pit in the seven feet. I saw shots fired that night not far from the gas in the low level. I believed it was my duty to examine the lamps, that is part of the duty of a fireman. I examined two lamps and the men said I might please myself whether I examined them; they had not been examined before. Both the lamps were unlocked. The men were Thomas Froggatt and either Joseph or Samuel Johnson. That was before the men entered on their work. I worked that night but not afterwards. I returned my keys, by my wife, to Charles Lawton. I saw several men and boys smoking. I did not return because I dare not. I had had enough while I was there. I did not dare return because there was so much gas in the mine, and no way of putting it out."

A Juror; - "That is your opinion?"

Mr. McDonald; – "And he saved his life by his opinion."

Witness; – "There was no way of putting out the gas at that time"

(To the deputy coroner) – "I have not been down the pit since and I do not know what has been done there since."

(To the jury) – "I never saw any rules to read. I know they ought to give out rules. I should think it is their place to put up the rules. I was not utterly regardless of what my duties were. It was not my duty to report the smoking to anybody above Lawton. Where I am I should smoke if I had the consent of the overman. I had no rules to read. Where I am I have read the rules though I am only a collier. It was my business to fire shots if I was sent for. I was not sent for while I was there. There were three shots fired in my station on the night of the 18th, as near as I can tell. The men fired themselves. I was there but they did not ask me to fire. Lawton did not tell me to fire, nor did he give me the rules."

The Coroner here explained that, by a previous statute, the proprietors of the pit were bound to supply rules to the men before allowing them to begin work, but under a subsequent statute that was repealed, and the proprietors were only bound to have the rules posted where the men could see them.

Mr. Wynne remarked that he urged the Government that it was undesirable to repeal that provision for the supply of rules to the men, and he much regretted that it had been repealed.

Witness (To the jury) – "I had no knowledge of the men having keys. I unscrewed the lamp, and lighted my pipe. I think there is no more danger in smoking than in lighting lamps. The pipe was lighted in the return air, close to the bottom of the pit."

(To Mr. Keary) – "I was deputy overman at Slappenhall Pit. There were rules there. I know what the duties of a fireman are. It is the duty of a fireman to see the place safe before firing shots. In trying the gas I put my lamp into it. It did not go out because I did not try it to that extent. I got my light for my pipe from the lamp, Lawton being by at the time. One of the men at work said the place was filling with gas. I tried to clear it but the place was not cleared. There were still two feet of gas over my head. I should have been out of my place in reporting the state of the pit to any of the managers. I left because my life was in danger. I did not tell Lawton the pit was dangerous, it would have been out of place to have instructed him in that manner. I worked there about six years ago. I have been in the office, and I have seen the rules, but I did not know what the rules were. I also smoked in the tunnel, and Lawton saw me there. I smoked more than twice, chiefly near the tunnel. I did not strike a match to light my pipe."

(To Mr. Wynne) – "I cannot tell where the air came into the jig. It would not be prudent at all times to take off the top of a lamp in the return air, sometimes it was safe to do it. I should not say anything if I saw a fireman open his lamp in the return air if it was safe."

William Jackson, brother of the previous witness, deposed; – "I was employed by Mr. Nicholls to work in the pit. I was engaged to work the day turn. Charles Lawton engaged my brother and he and I went to Mr. Nicholls. It was in September. I followed my brother on the Monday. On that day Lawton took me to see the gas in the low level. Part of my work was in the low level and part in the new seven foot. I saw gas on that day. I went again the next morning – Tuesday. The low level I then considered worse. It was filled with gas and was stopped totally. Nicholas Fletcher stopped the work. I was ordered to break the brattices beyond the second place, fifteen yards back, and hang a drop sheet beyond the second place. I found gas all that day in the level. If both the sheets were down it would alter the ventilation, but I don't recollect both being down. I saw smoking in the mine while I was there. I did not go back after the 18th. The parties are dead who I saw smoking. Dutton, the doggy, was one. I saw my brother Enoch smoking in the presence of Charles Lawton. Shots were fired by the men themselves. No one ordered me to fire them that I can recollect. I had two reasons for not returning to work. It was work I had not been accustomed to, the other reason for not returning was that I did not think it was safe. I was afraid, not so much on account of the quantity of gas but on account of the smoking."

(To the jury) – "By order of Nicholas Fletcher there were no shots fired in the second brow. It was so full of gas. Smoking was commoner than I liked. I never heard anybody say that the men were not to smoke. I did not see any lamps unlocked or any with their tops off. A fan was put down to drive the air off the second brow but it did not do it."

(To Mr. Keary) – "I worked there seven years ago. I then had a copy of the rules. I went on the second night to Nicholls to get my discharge. The only reason I gave him was that I was not used to the work. I did not say anything about smoking. Nicholls was present at the time Dutton was smoking. That was in the middle level. Nicholls made no remark about the smoking. I never saw a pipe lighted. I considered it was dangerous to stay there. It was equally dangerous for others to stay.

(To Mr. McDonald) – "The reason why I gave that excuse to Nicholls was to get my liberty. I had no further reason."

John Kent deposed; – "I am a collier. I live in New Road. I have worked in North Staffordshire Colliery. I saw smoking there, and have smoked myself. I have never lit my pipe at Lawton's lamp. I left in consequence of the explosion. I had been afraid before the explosion. I was afraid when the gas was fired by Draycott some time before the explosion in December, it was about a month before."

(To the deputy coroner) – "It was the firing of a shot that caused it. Draycott worked no more after then."

(To the jury) – "I had a key to open my lamp but I threw it away. I have fired twenty shots without sending for the fireman. I was never cautioned. I have taken my lamp top off to get a light to fire my shots. If the fireman was there he would fire the shots."

(To Mr. Keary) – "I once complained to Fletcher about the gas and the ventilation was altered. I left on account of a quarrel with another man. That was a fortnight before the explosion. Draycott was turned away for firing the shot. I never was cautioned by anyone not to fire shots."

(To Mr. McDonald) – "The pit was as usual the night before the explosion. Fletcher never came with a book to take down what was said about the gas when men complained."

(To Mr. Wynne) – "I believe I have told one person that I lighted my pipe at Lawton's lamp. I cannot recollect that I have lighted my pipe at Lawton's lamp. I may have done so."

(To Mr. McDonald) – "We got the powder in the pit. I bought it from Lawton. That was the practice in the pit."

(To a juror, Mr. Dixon) – "I have had some conversation as to powder during the adjournment for refreshment, the conversation was with that fellow (pointing to Mr. McDonald)."

(To Mr. Keary) – "The powder was kept in an opening in the coal made on purpose. It was given out in tins four or five pounds at a time."

(To the jury); – "The money for the powder was stopped by Nicholls. I have seen others supplied by Lawton with powder. I never tried to take down powder bought anywhere else. I have seen three or four getting powder at one time in the pit. It was a general thing for men to take powder in that way. Men have complained."

Mr. Keary said that Mr. McDonald was now going into irrelevant matter. It was quite irrelevant how the powder was bought and paid for.

A juror observed that it was worthy of consideration whether 6 or 7 cwt. of powder was kept in the pit to supply the men.

Mr. Keary submitted that a store of powder could have had nothing to do with the explosion, as all the cans had been sent up empty on the morning of the explosion.

Mr. Wynne to witness; – "Have you seen barrels of powder go down?"

Witness; – "No it was in cans."

Samuel Highfield deposed; – "I worked for the North Staffordshire Coal Company about four months before the accident. I worked in the eight foot and in the seven foot at day work. I saw gas in the seven foot, in several places up at the facings. I went from the seven foot to the eight foot to mend myself. I was not frightened from it."

The Coroner having asked Mr. McDonald if he had any more witnesses ready, and having received a negative reply, said that it was an extreme hardship upon the gentlemen of the jury, after having adjourned solely for Mr. McDonald to produce evidence, to remain there and have no witness produced.

Mr. McDonald observed that he should be quite satisfied to close there, for the other evidence he had hoped to produce would only be a repetition of what the jury had heard.

The Coroner remarked that it had been intimated to him that, unless Mr. McDonald had evidence to carry on his case, it was a hardship to sit there and do nothing.

Mr. McDonald granted that is was so, adding that his other witnesses were absent through a mistake.

The Coroner said that Mr. McDonald had had a week at least to prepare his evidence.

William Ramsay was here stated to be present, and was called. He said; – "I am fireman to the North Staffordshire Coal Company. I am still working for the company and work in the ten foot. I have not worked in the seven foot".

Mr. McDonald, on hearing the last reply did not pursue the information.

Mr. Wynne said he was not going to call any more witnesses; therefore the inquiry was virtually at an end.

The Coroner asked Mr. McDonald if he had anything more to say

Mr. McDonald; – "I wish to state the cause of my being here."

Deputy Coroner; – "You say the other persons you have named as witnesses would only support the evidence you have already given?"

Mr. McDonald; – "Just so"

The Coroner; – "If you think the witnesses you have in view can give important evidence, I would submit it to the jury to grant you further time; but at present I don't see that you have furnished anything more than a repetition of what we have had over and over again."

Deputy Coroner; – "We have had nothing today but what we have had before."

Mr. McDonald; – "The additional evidence would simply be as to the state of the mine prior to the explosion, and I think we have had enough of that today."

The Coroner; – "I understood you that you wished to make a statement."

Mr. Keary observed that he withdrew his objection, on condition that Mr. McDonald would confine himself to the evidence before the jury.

Mr. McDonald said that the reason for his presence was that Mr. Wynne had written to him respecting an expression of his, such expression being based on the result of certain enquiries made through the agency of an association of which he had the honour to be President. He found, from the public reports, that the resulting statement had been declared to be untrue. He alluded to the statement that the mine had been, during some months previously, in a highly explosive condition, and that the men had been liable at any moment to be blown to pieces. It had been said that his information had been derived from persons on the spot, and one gentleman had, he believed, been blamed for communicating information to him. He wished to state that that gentleman had, neither directly nor indirectly, given him the slightest information.

The Foreman; – "Will you have the kindness to name?"

Mr. McDonald continued; – The name of the gentleman was Mr. Hickman, whom he had not asked a single question. The information had been gathered by an officer of an association, one of whose objects was to secure an alteration of the law under which Mr. Wynne was an inspector. He (Mr. McDonald) had that day shown recklessness and want of care; that the mine was in a state disgraceful to a civilised country; of management there was none. They found a powder shop in it, and everything tended to show a total disregard of order, regularity, and law in the colliery. He thanked the gentlemen of the jury for the patience they had displayed that day.

Mr. Wynne; – "I did not charge Mr. McDonald with stating a falsehood, but what I said was the statement he made was true or false, and, if true, it ought to be proved.

Mr. Dixon, a juror; – "Allow me to say that when Mr. McDonald's letter was read, I remarked that, according to the evidence so far, the statement was not correct. I think then that it is not fair to have such a statement as this (holding up a small bill) circulated. This bill gives what has been printed in a newspaper."

The inquiry as to the lamentable accident at Talke, in North Staffordshire, is proceeding, having been adjourned from today until the 31st inst. The evidence adduced so far gives great force to the glaring defect which has been pointed out in inspector's reports in these letters, and in other ways, in the working of mines in Staffordshire, namely, *the want of discipline.* The mine, especially parts of it, was liable to frequent emissions of gas very variable in amount. The further evidence taken at the inquest proves that Mr. McDonald's statement as to the habitually dangerous state of the mine was substantially correct; and it is much to be regretted that the Miners' Union officers did not think it worth their while to lodge a formal complaint with the government inspector, which could have been referred to in case an accident afterwards occurred, and, which would, no doubt, in this case, have been the means of saving a fearful sacrifice of life. Mr. McDonald remarks in his letter to Mr. Wynne that, "should the jury be all of the stamp of the one that roared out when you mentioned my statement, then the verdict is known already", and, judging from the circumstance that the foreman of the jury (the Rev. M. W. McHutchin) has positively stated, that he is intimate with Mr. Johnson, the manager, and, that the jury loudly applauded (by stamping their feet and otherwise)

anything said by a witness in favour of the manager and underground bailiff, their verdict, whatever it may be, will not be worth the paper it is written upon. It is difficult to understand --- *(undiscipherable)* --- The question to be faced was whether --- *(undiscipherable)* -- was guilty of manslaughter. The evidence adduced has revealed a system of recklessness and incompetency in management greatly deplorable and it is to be regretted that there is not, as in the case of similar experiences as this, a legal mode of publicly degrading those so unwisely entrusted with power.

The mine was known to be fiery yet the whole ventilation was guided by a single door. The air was brought down 300 feet after passing through the workings, but in the opinion of Mr. Coe, colliery manager for Mr. Robert Heath, it did not, in this particular case, argue any want of skill. The miners were allowed to brush out the gas from their working places, and the firemen re-lighted lamps in the return air, yet "taking all circumstances into consideration," Mr. Coe "would have carried on the workings in the same way they were carried on." Heaven protect us from working in a pit managed by Mr. Coe or Mr. Johnson!

Mr. Hickman rose and commenced speaking, but was stopped, not before claiming exoneration from the charges under which he had laboured.

Mr. Keary then addressed the jury; – It was quite right, he observed, that when a fearful catastrophe like that they had met to inquire into occurred, that the management should, to some extent, be placed on their trial, and it was the duty of the Coroner, still more of the jury, to investigate narrowly the management of the place where the dreadful accident had occurred, so as to ascertain if the managers had been the cause of the accident in any way, and they were bound to enquire whether the management had been proper, and whether the managers had, in any way, discouraged those who had complaints to make. Tried by these tests he believed that the gentlemen he represented were entitled to be acquitted at the hands of the jury. he did not mean the owners, who lived at a distance but more particularly Mr. Johnson and Mr. Nicholls, who were really responsible, Mr. Nicholls more immediately so. The jury had seen that Nicholls was a person of skill and intelligence. He had held his present situation ten years, and responsible positions for twenty-two years, and *prima facie* was a person of skill and experience. The evidence of scientific witnesses showed that the works had been laid out skilfully and properly, and that credit was due to the managers. Proper rules had been made to secure the safety of the men, and of these he would read a few bearing on the subject of the inquiry. – The purport of the rules read was that the managers were expressly ordered to give their first attention to the safety of the lives and limbs of those in the pit; the firemen were to examine the workings every morning an hour before the men went to work; the workmen were prohibited working anywhere that gas was present; they were prohibited from firing shots without express permission; smoking was prohibited, as also was the use of false keys, and if, continued Mr. Keary, the rules had been attended to, the accident could never have occurred. Although forty witnesses had been examined there was no proof that either Mr. Johnson or Mr. Nicholls was cognisant of breaches of the rules, except in one case and in that case the man had been immediately discharged. It had also been proved that, from other parts of the same colliery, men had been summoned for offences and had been fined. What more could be done? Colliers, and not colliers alone, as had been proved in Regent's Park, seemed to be utterly regardless of danger, and in no occupation was more truly verified the old proverb, "Familiarity breeds contempt." Mr. McDonald's statement that the explosion could have taken place at any moment was not borne out by the evidence, and it was but justice to say that the two witnesses called by Mr. McDonald that the explosion had had the effect of magnifying the danger in their eyes, for they never would have left a hundred of their fellow creatures in imminent danger of their lives without uttering some warning. He had no doubt that the explosion occurred in the up-brow, and a good deal of criticism had been passed by the inspector upon the way in which the works had been laid out. At an early stage of the inquiry, Mr. Wynne seemed to think that the back dip ought to have been cleared out, but a very satisfactory explanation of why it had not been so treated had been

given. Mr. Nicholls had said that he thought it better to drive the up-brow, and every witness had confirmed that opinion. Nicholls had pushed on with all possible speed in order to make the communication. With regard to the door in the main jig, Mr. Wynne had said at first that there ought to have been two, but when Nicholls pointed out the shortness of the distance, and that if there had been two doors they would be practically open at the same time, Mr. Wynne agreed with him, but suggested that there ought to have been two sheets instead of one door, but then Mr. McDonald had brought out two sheets as a great grievance, and the evidence showed that they did not answer, as they were torn down and stopped the air. He had no wish to undervalue Mr. Wynne's opinion, but he could not help remarking that all the witnesses were against him, when he said that it was not safe to drive the level, and this led him to observe that though Nicholls, who was not infallible, might have committed an error in judgement, he had exercised a sound discretion, in which he was supported by the testimony of gentlemen of great experience. It was doubtless a hard word to use against the men who were killed, but no doubt the explosion had been caused by their recklessness. Mr. Nicholls and Mr. Johnson felt very acutely for all those who had suffered and he hoped the jury would not inflict upon their memory the stigma of censure, and he confidently asked the jury not to cast any aspersions on either Mr. Nicholls or Mr. Johnson.

Mr. Wynne stated that his opinion was unchanged that the back brow ought to have been cleared out, and that nothing should have been done while there was only one air course, but what was absolutely necessary. He wished also to explain that he did not think it was proper to have two sheets, but that two sheets were better than one door.

The Coroner, in summing up, expressed the hope that the verdict which the jury were about to give would give satisfaction to the county at large. The question for the jury to consider was, first, how these unfortunate men came by their death, and on that there could not be two opinions, an explosion having resulted from an accumulation of gas. – After reading the law as to responsibility for such occurrences, the Coroner added – that if an underground bailiff acted in a reckless manner in the discharge of his duty, and was aware that what he was doing was careless and reckless, if death ensued, he was guilty of manslaughter, though no man, it had been held could be indicted for that offence, if he had only been guilty of an error of judgement, if he acted for the best, in his judgement; but if a person in a position of trust was guilty of gross neglect, then, in case of death resulting he was indictable. He asked the jury, then, to decide whether, in their judgement, Nicholls – he left Mr. Johnson out of the question – had been guilty of reckless conduct in the discharge of his duties, or whether they thought he had acted to the best of his skill and ability. If the parties who had been at work in the mine had been alive, one question for the jury would have been whether Lissamore, who had been found with a pipe in his hand near the place where the explosion had occurred had not been guilty of such a breach of the rules as would have made him criminally responsible. Unfortunately he, and others, had lost their lives, and he only referred to the circumstance as showing the recklessness and carelessness that had prevailed in the pit, and that on many separate occasions the pit had been found free from gas. On the other hand they had two witnesses, called by Mr. McDonald, who said they left in consequence of the gas. There was some contradiction in the evidence of the scientific witnesses on this point, but it was clear that, unless there had been a great quantity of gas, the explosion would not have occurred. How came the gas there? In Mr. Wynne's judgement, the works were not skilfully carried on. It was for the jury to decide the whole question, and he trusted their verdict would have the effect of preventing such accidents in the future. The inquiry was a national one, and he thought he should have done wrong if, presiding over so important an inquiry, he had not acceded to the request of Mr. McDonald. He much regretted that remarks had been made about the jury, for he was satisfied that they would do their duty. – The Coroner closed with remarks complimentary to those who had gone to the rescue of their fellow creatures in the pit, and of those who had contributed liberally to the support of the families.

The jury then retired to deliberate, and, after an absence of an hour and a half returned with the following:

VERDICT

We find that Nicholas Fletcher and ninety others met their deaths by an explosion of gas in the North Staffordshire Coal and Iron Company's Banbury mine on 13th December last. No positive evidence has been brought before us to show how the accident occurred but we are of the opinion that an accumulation of gas had taken place in some of the lower workings, in consequence of the upsetting of a train of coals in a doorway, and the gas, coming in contact with a naked light unlawfully exposed by one of the miners, exploded. We find that if the rules and regulations made by the managers of the pit had been carried out, as they ought to have been by their subordinates, the explosion might not have taken place. We regret to see the culpable negligence shown by James Bossons and Charles Lawton in violating the rules made for the protection of life and property in the pit. We should suggest that means be adopted by Mr. Nicholls, the underground bailiff of the mine, for carrying out more strictly the rules of the pit, with regard to the men firing their own shots, brushing out the gas themselves, smoking pipes and re-lighting their lamps in the return air. We cannot urge too strongly on the Government the necessity of appointing additional inspectors of mines.

The Coroner said that the effect of the verdict was that the deceased persons had come by their death accidentally.

The foreman gave an affirmative reply.

This closed the inquiry which had been thoroughly exhaustive, and in the course of which a desire has been manifested by all concerned to bring out every fact which could be of the slightest use in enabling the jury to arrive at a correct decision.

CHAPTER EIGHT
KEATES AND FORD'S DIRECTORY
LOCAL REVIEW OF THE YEAR — 1866

TALKE MINING DISASTER

The district had not recovered from the horror excited by the news of the colliery catastrophe at Barnsley, when it was itself visited by a calamity, less terrible in its results than that at Barnsley, but the most appalling which has marked the history of mining in North Staffordshire. On the morning of the 13th December, some 134 men and boys went into the Big Banbury Pit, at Talke (the property of the North Staffordshire Coal and Iron Company), to work, at their usual hour. Two thirds of the number went into the south workings, where a fine seam of seven foot Banbury coal, highly charged with gas, had been recently discovered, and was being, after a large outlay of capital, advantageously worked. At half-past eleven o'clock in the day an explosion of gas took place in this part of the mine. A minute after eighty-nine men and boys were corpses strewed in all directions in the pit; thirteen were lying senseless; fourteen horses were struck dead, and their stable was on fire. The explosion shook the earth like an earthquake for half a mile round; dense masses of smoke and dust rolled up the shaft, and filled the atmosphere with a thick fog. These were the signs visible above the surface of the destruction which had been effected below. Only too well aware of the nature, though not of the extent, of what had occurred, and calm and collected, as the emergency required, the managers of the pit and the men at hand, as soon as the smoke had cleared away, began the work of rescuing those who were within reach of human aid. Some fifty men, who were at work on the north side of the pit, and heard the report of the explosion roll like thunder through the narrow avenues of the mine, at once hurried to the shaft, and were drawn up unhurt. A few of those who were on the other side escaped almost by a miracle, and came safely to the surface. The news of the accident quickly spread, and ere long colliers from neighbouring pits, and then, in rapid succession, experienced mining engineers and colliery managers from all parts of the district, came to offer their services in the dangerous and merciful labour of rescuing the still living sufferers. When the first party of brave volunteers reached the bottom of the mine they came upon a scene which no pen can describe, corpses lay in all directions – in some places in heaps. The majority had died a peaceful death from suffocation by "after-damp", but the remainder had been burnt, and some were frightfully disfigured and mutilated. Two or three lay with their heads partially blown off, and were beyond the recognition of friends, except by marks on the body. In these chambers of horrors the searching parties pursued their work of mercy, some of their members having to be brought to the surface after a time, drunk with the fatal vapour that still filled the pit and from the effects of inhaling which they were only recovered by being rapidly walked about in the open air. One by one black inanimate objects were brought out of the pit, briefly examined by one, or more, of several surgeons in attendance, to see if life was extinct, and one after another were carried away to the neighbouring inn to be washed and laid out. All day, and far into the night, the drawing up of bodies went on, and when this was suspended to allow some necessary repairs to the ventilation of the pit to be effected, fifty-eight corpses had been recovered. During all this time the scene at the pit bank was of the most harrowing description. Around the head of the shaft stood a dense crowd of colliers and others looking sadly and silently on the terrible revelations of the catastrophe. At the edge of the bank were men and women anxiously enquiring for sons, brothers or husbands, whose corpses would presently pass them on the way to the inn. At the latter place a still more heart-rending tragedy was being enacted. There dead bodies were being identified by friends and relatives frantic in their grief. All through the dull afternoon, the dark evening, the cold and bitter night, these things were going on, and when the next morning arrived fifty-eight bodies were decently laid out at the inn, ready to be placed in their coffins. When night came again the examination of the mine was resumed, and before morning twenty-four more human corpses had been brought out of the pit. Then the search was again suspended to allow the ventilation of the pit to be restored, and one of the pipes of the pump, which had burst, to be repaired. The latter work occupied nearly a week, but in the interval the carcasses of the horses were brought up and buried; further investigation of the workings had been made without result; but, by accident, the men employed in restoring the bratticing discovered four men lying dead behind a sheet, on the Wednesday, and the same day two other bodies were found near the bottom of the shaft, where they were supposed to have floated from the "sump". Of the thirteen men and boys rescued alive two afterwards died, making 91 deaths as the amount of the fatality caused by the explosion. For several days after the catastrophe the colliery was the centre of great excitement. Thousands of people from the neighbouring towns and villages visited the colliery and the inn where the dead bodies lay. On the Sunday after the explosion the main street of the village was scarcely passable for the crowds. On the afternoon of that day the remains of twenty-two of the victims were consigned to their resting place in Talke churchyard, and as many more bodies were interred in various churchyards in the neighbourhood. The next day twenty-one more were buried in Talke, the next day following

three more, and the day after that another six, and in the intervening days the rest of the dead were deposited in the earth in other localities. The catastrophe was from the first suspected to be due to carelessness on the part of some of the men employed in the pit, and the subsequent investigation has shown this supposition to be correct; but the blame does not rest wholly with the workmen, and is shared to a grave extent by those who had charge of the mine. Though no less than twenty-seven false lamp keys were found on many dead, and though the under officials of the pit knew that men smoked while at work they never, on their own admission, attempted to prevent the unlocking of lamps, or to check smoking; and though firing of shots by the men was prohibited, and men were appointed to do this duty, the rule was systematically neglected. The precise actual cause of the accident will probably never be known, but that it was one of three – the firing of shots, smoking, or removing the top of a lamp – is pretty conclusively established. The ventilation of the pit, too, according to the Government Inspector of Mines was defective, and a grave error had been committed by the management in driving new workings while the ventilation was imperfect. The pit was declared to be free of gas on the morning of the accident, except in one place, where it was cleared away at once, and to have been generally sufficiently ventilated to prevent any large accumulation of gas. In blind trust to chance, shots were fired in the night preceding the explosion, and evidence of smoking and of lamps being unlocked on the very day of the accident was found in the subsequent discovery of two lamps unlocked and another with the head removed, in the pit, one of the corpses held a half-smoked pipe in his hand. Pipes and tobacco boxes were found on more than a dozen of the dead men, and lucifer matches on most of them. Considering the gaseous nature of the coal, the clearly proved occasional presence of gas, in the shape of blowers, the neglect of duty by those in charge of the workings, and the recklessness of the colliers themselves, the wonder is not that the explosion occurred, but that it did not take place before. While it appears clear that the systematic neglect of rules on the part of the colliers and overmen was unknown to the

managers, it is also clear that they adopted no means of periodically ascertaining the state of the pit, and whether the rules were carried out or not. By this calamity 181 persons who had been dependent upon the victims were thrown destitute upon the world. The number includes 37 widows, 81 children, eight parents supported by sons, 11 orphans, 8 parents partially supported, 13 men injured, and 23 dependent on men injured. A public subscription for the relief of these sufferers was at once opened, Mr. Smith Child heading the list with £500 and the Queen following with a gift of £100. In most of the towns and villages of North Staffordshire funds were started, and at the same time a subscription was opened at the Mansion House, London, for sufferers at Talke and Barnsley.

After an inquiry, lasting eight days, the coroner's jury returned a verdict of accidental death, with the addition that no positive evidence to show how the accident had occurred had been brought before them, but they were of the opinion that an accumulation of gas had taken place in some of the lower workings in consequence of the upsetting of a train of coals in the air-way, and the gas exploded on coming in contact with a naked light unlawfully exposed by one of the miners. They found that if the rules and regulations of the pit had been carried out, as they ought to have been, by the subordinate officials, the explosion might not have taken place. The jury regretted to see culpable negligence by a fireman, and an underlooker named* and suggested that means be adopted, by the managers, of carrying out more strictly the rules of the pit with regard to the men firing their own shots, brushing away gas themselves, smoking, and re-lighting their lamps in the air-way. The jury added that they could not too strongly urge upon the Government the necessity for the appointment of additional inspectors of mines.

Up to the end of January the amount received by the treasurer of the Relief Committee was nearly £7,800, in addition to which about £2,300 had been raised by local funds in different parts of the district but had not been paid over to the general treasurer. The amount required for the relief of the sufferers was estimated at, at least, £15,000. At the date already named some £20,000 had been sent to the Lord Mayor and one fifth of the Mansion House fund was expected to be sent to Talke. Assistance is also being raised in South Staffordshire, Birmingham, and other places, and at the former place, at the end of January, £2,269, and at Birmingham £1,667 had been received on account of both casualties. From all these sources the amount required for Talke may be expected to be obtained in the course of a short time but the relief committee are anxious to have a surplus with which to set on foot a permanent relief fund for those left without support in future colliery accidents. It is doubtful whether this scheme can be carried out judging from the present position of the relief fund and the slowness with which subscriptions have latterly been coming in.

---

* Bossons was the fireman and Charles Lawton the underlooker.

CHAPTER NINE

STAFFORDSHIRE SENTINEL LETTERS FEBRUARY 1867

TALKE ACCIDENT

Letter No. 1
To the Editor of the Staffordshire
Sentinel.

5th February 1867

Sir, – My attention has been called to a letter published in the Sentinel of Saturday last, signed George Shenton, Primitive Methodist Schoolmaster, Talk-o'-th'-Hill, calling upon me to produce my authority for certain statements alleged to have been made with reference to the status of Mr. Shenton in the above matter, or to recall such statements, and in reply I have determined to give you the facts in their order. I may state, in passing, that I attended the first meeting of the Relief Committee, but, in consequence of the subsequent meetings being held in the middle of the day, I was unable to attend them. I was informed, I think on the 16th January last, by the Rev. William Harley, a member of the committee, that the Rev. M.W.McHutchin had offered Mr. Shenton £3, in payment for services rendered by him and that, as Mr. Shenton considered the amount insufficient, he (Mr.

Harley) had been requested to bring the matter before the committee at their next meeting, and try to obtain for Mr. Shenton an additional sum. I at once explained to Mr. Harley that payments such as these could not be made out of the fund, and, believing at the time that Mr. Shenton was not a person likely either to claim, or accept, if rendered, any portion of the funds at the disposal of the committee, I wrote him on the day following Letter No. 1 in which I distinctly told him that I did not believe the report. In reply to this I received what I considered an insulting scrap of paper, asking me how many times I had attended the committee meetings, which I did not notice, and later in the day I received the strange production numbered 2. I was quite unable to understand this further than that Mr. Shenton either had received, or expected to receive, some remuneration for his services from the accident fund and I wrote him letter numbered 3, to which he has not yet replied. I was not at this time aware of what had taken place between Mr. Shenton and Mr. McHutchin as to £3 having been offered, and it was only last evening that I obtained the particulars from Mr. McHutchin with permission to make use of them in this letter. Mr. McHutchin met Mr. Shenton, I believe accidentally, and asked him if he wished his services to be mentioned to the committee, with a view to his being remunerated and he said he did. Mr. McHutchin, subsequent to this, had a conversation with a member of the committee, who, entertaining an impression that it was scarcely the kind of claim to be made on the widows' and orphans' fund, requested Mr. McHutchin to offer Mr. Shenton £3, and told him that, if the committee could not allow the payment, he would pay the money out of his own pocket. Mr. McHutchin offered the £3 to Mr. Shenton who said, "No, I cannot take this." Mr. McHutchin, supposing that the sum was considered too large, then offered £2, upon which Mr. Shenton said, "I do not mean that; £5 would not repay me." In about half an hour afterwards Mr. Shenton came to Mr. McHutchin and told him that £10 would not repay him, upon which Mr. McHutchin said, "I cannot give you £10, and I must

bring the matter before the committee." Mr. McHutchin brought the matter before the committee at their meeting held on the 22nd. ult., as agreed upon with Mr. Shenton, and the members of the committee unanimously decided that such a claim could not be entertained.

I might leave your readers to form their own opinion upon these facts, whether my statements were "unfounded" or not, but I am not disposed to part with Mr. Shenton so easily. What does he mean by, "bill of claim"? Surely he does not intend to insult the understanding of your readers by supposing that they will not consider a claim to have been made unless a "bill of claim" was written out and delivered. It would have been very difficult to discover from the letter published in your column that Mr. Shenton had anything to do with the occupation of schoolmaster, if he had not so described himself, but a similar difficulty would not have presented itself in supposing that the "bill of claim" was a remnant of the grocer's shop. That he did assent to the claim being made, I think, abundantly appears. First, from the permission accorded to Mr. McHutchin to bring the matter before the committee; secondly, from the letter No. 2, written four days before the meeting of the committee, in which, it will be observed that he underlines the word "must" near the end of it which, to my mind, is making a claim in the strongest sense of the word; and thirdly, from the fact of a request having been made to Mr. Harley, a member of the committee, by a friend of Mr. Shenton's to ask the committee to allow something beyond the £3 tendered.

I admit that Mr. Shenton rendered cheerful assistance at the time of the accident, but others did so too, and, except in the case of a few workmen and women, no claim for services rendered has been made. One person, whose efforts had been untiring, being asked if he had any claim to make, replied, "No; if the committee offered me anything I would put as much to it and give it to the fund." and, with the solitary exception before your readers, this has been the feeling of everyone. Even Police Constable Beckett, whose exertions were particularly praiseworthy, was not allowed to receive a gratuity from the fund, and I challenge Mr. Shenton to name a single person in a position at all equal with his own who has asked for or received a penny. I leave it to your readers to say whether my conclusions are so "tremendously faulty" as Mr. Shenton pretends to suppose, and whether a statement as to a claim having been made or sanctioned by him were "groundless and unfounded". Although, as far as I am concerned, the fact of such a claim having been made, whether authorised or not, completely exonerates me, yet I waive this, and accepting the issue raised, assert that such a claim was made or sanctioned by Mr. Shenton. I do not consider it at all a "dangerous career" to "tempt the displeasure" of Mr. Shenton, and I shall be happy to discuss in your columns, as long as you think it desirable, to bring before the public a purely private matter. I have been on friendly terms with Mr. Shenton for years, and you will easily perceive that in writing to him letter No 1, I was only anxious to extricate him, if I could, from what appeared to me to be a most unenviable position. If you afford me the opportunity of again addressing you in the matter by inserting another letter from Mr. Shenton, I shall feel inclined to ask him how he makes it possible for a "blush" to "dimple" a modest face, and what amount of "perseverence" and "zeal" it would have required to have gotten at his "pocket" and his "means" for the benefit of these poor widows and orphans. It seems to me that he exercised both perseverence and zeal to get £10 from the pockets of the poor sufferers, and he will scarcely be able, I think, to escape from his disagreeable position by imposing upon your readers the impossible task of understanding such phrases as "outersides", "ludicrously solemn" and the other nonsense which forms a considerable portion of his letter.

I am, sir, your obedient servant,

THOS. SHERRAT
Talk-o'-th'-Hill, February 5th 1867.

Letter No.1 — To Mr. Shenton.
Talk on the Hill, near Lawton Cheshire
January 17th 1867
My dear sir, – The Rev. Mr. Harley has just informed me that you have been offered, or received, £3 for some services rendered in this matter, and that a request has been preferred to him to ask for a further sum from the committee. I told Mr. Harley that I
did not think you would have a penny, as you are a person of independent means, and I believe the report to be entirely without foundation. I know that you were very kind in washing, &ct., and that your school may have been, in consequence, closed for a time, but in a matter where everyone is contributing something in money, and some persons their valuable time, I cannot think that you would condescend to make such a claim. You know how anxious I am, at any time, to do anything for you, but I must say that if any such claim as that, as to £3 paid, or any further sum to be allowed, is brought before the committee, I shall oppose it with all my might. I have just written Mr. McHutchin telling him what I have heard, and that I do not believe it. I have also told him that, as a member of the committee, I object to the payment of any sum of money, except to the widows and persons in whose favour the amount has been subscribed. I have been pained and surprised more than I can tell you by the report. – Yours faithfully,

Thos. Sherratt

Letter No. 2 — To Mr Sherratt

Coal Pit Hill Day School
January 18th 1867

My dear sir, – By this time I trust you have heard from Mr. McHutchin and that you are now in a position to look at me, "the reports" the Rev. Mr. Harley, also yourself, and the epistle of this morning as a member of the committee I think you are and have been somewhat relax in your attentions thereon, or very indifferent when there and in Council. I think you have not been many time's, if any at all, if you have why have you not stopt the monies paid by sanction of that said committee to persons I could name. Rev. M.W. McHutchin can tell you all but as a member of the committee you should know, and if you knew, why did you and the rest sanction and if sanction, why complain if a man possesses "independent means", query that excludes him from consideration, as to deservings with the rest of the workers I think your deductions are tremendiously faulty but I think your attention to committee duties far worse really my dear sir I dont know how to look at you as a "member" of the committee and your letter to me of this morning but supposing I was of "independent means" does it

follow that I must devote my time neglect my school duties, and for three days and three nights attend the dead, and through this require the attention of the "Doctor" for a fortnight and have to pay him. I think if any of the workers must be paid and they have been, I must when I began I had no idea of pay, and if you as a "member" of the committee can so reduce the question to pay, I can "condescend" to receive my "penny." – I am, faithfully,
    GEO. SHENTON

Letter No. 3 — To Mr. Shenton.
Talk-on-the-Hill, near Lawton, Cheshire
January 18th 1867

My dear sir, – I have only been able to attend one meeting of the committee and I cannot therefore tell who has been paid for services rendered. I will, however, attend on Tuesday, and know something more about the matter. I cannot make anything at all of your letter just received, further than that you either have received, or expect to receive, some remuneration for your services. I again tell you that I am both surprised and sorry at this, and, no reasons to be advanced can remove from my mind this impression. I am quite prepared to understand that some persons who assisted would expect remuneration, but I should really have thought that if you had rendered any services they would have been gratuitous. I do not for a moment believe that you do not sympathise with those who have suffered, and yet I cannot understand how this sympathy has been evidenced, when not only is your name "found absent" from the list of subscriptions, but you actually seek to diminish a fund already sadly deficient, to compensate you for personal loss and inconvenience. I have only attended one meeting of the committee, and £5 is all the money that I have contributed, but I have assisted those in distress in very many other ways. How many days do you suppose Mr. McHutchin has devoted to the object? He cannot better afford it than you can, and yet he has not only not claimed for services rendered, but has given £3 to the fund. I cannot help again telling you that I am deeply pained at what has taken place as far as you are concerned, because it must have the effect of lowering you in the estimation of the public. I have not heard from Mr. McHutchin in reply to my letter. – Yours faithfully,

Thos. Sherratt

CHAPTER TEN
BRITISH PARLIAMENTARY PAPERS 1867
REPORTS TO THE SECRETARY OF STATE FOR THE HOME DEPARTMENT

EXTRACT FROM INDEX UNDER LETTER "T"
OF REPORT, 1867 FROM
SELECT COMMITTEE ON MINES

Talk-of-the-Hill Colliery.

Information relative to the composition of the jury on the occasion of the coroner's inquest after the explosion at this colliery in December 1866, *Wynne* 694-714. 794-797——Unsatisfactory conduct of the jury at one period of the inquiry, so that the coroner considered it necessary to reprove them, *ib*. 715-729. 793. 797-801——Unfavourable opinion formed by witnesses of the part taken by Mr. Johnson and Mr. Nicholls in the management of the mine; desire in the locality to exempt the former from all blame, *ib*. 730-738. 797-800.

Conclusion that the explosion was owing to bad management, and that inspection would not have guarded against it unless the inspector had paid frequent visits, and had been in the mine a week or so before the accident. *Wynne* 738-757. 778-791. 802-806——Good ventilation of that part of the mine which was opened when inspected by witness about a year before the accident, *ib*. 747-749——Circumstance of a consulting engineer having been appointed to the Talk-of-the-Hill colliery, Mr. Johnson and Mr. Nicholls being however still continued in employment, *ib*. 770-778——Absence of any actions for damages against Mr. Nichols (sic) or Mr. Johnson; liberality displayed towards the widows and orphans adverted to hereon, *ib*. 777. 806-808.

Conclusion that the Talk-of-the-Hill explosion arose from the want of discipline and of good management, and that it would not have been prevented by previous or frequent inspection, *Evans* 864-873. 917-923——Limited extent of the workings at the time of the accident, *ib*. 873. 934-937——Satisfactory conduct, on the whole, of the jury on the occasion of the Talk-of-the-Hill inquiry, *ib*. 884-886.

Statement by the inspectors as to the accident having been attributable to neglect and laxity of discipline, *App*. 64.

APPENDIX No.2

COAL MINES (ACCIDENTS AND EXPLOSIONS)

ANSWERS OF INSPECTORS

COPY of a CIRCULAR LETTER from the Home Office to, and REPORTS from, the Inspectors of Mines to the Secretary of State to the Home Department, on the recent ACCIDENTS and EXPLOSIONS in COAL MINES; together with the LETTER of INSTRUCTIONS of the 29th day of January 1867, from the Secretary of State for the Home Department to Mr. *Southern* the recently appointed Inspector of Mines.

No.1

CIRCULAR

Sir,   Whitehall, 26th December 1866

UNDERSTANDING that a meeting of the Government mines inspectors is likely to take place on the 23rd January next, preparatory to their making a separate and distinct report in writing of each of their proceedings during the preceding year, and seeing that such report will not in the ordinary course of business be presented to Parliament before the 1st March 1867, Mr. Walpole is extremely anxious, in consequence of the fearful and calamitous accidents which have recently occurred, that you should take that opportunity of conferring together for the purpose of considering whether additional means might not at once be devised, for preventing, if possible, the recurrence, or at all events for diminishing the risk, of such and the like accidents in future.

The approaching inquests will probably furnish you with valuable information upon some points, which may properly be brought under the immediate attention of Parliament, and Mr. Walpole has therefore to request that you will be so good as to take this matter into your early consideration, so that he may have, before Parliament meets, your joint opinion thereupon in writing, with such suggestions for the improvement of the law as your knowledge of the subject and your long experience, aided by the inquiries to which I have adverted,

may enable you to offer.
I have etc,
(signed) *Belmore*

.

Joseph Dickinson, Esq.
Inspector of Mines.

No. 2
REPORT From The
Inspectors Of Coal Mines.

Sir,   London 26th January 1867
THE inspectors of coal mines have the honour to acknowledge the receipt of the Earl of Belmore's circular letter of the 26th ult., relative to the fearfully calamitous accidents which have recently occurred. In obedience to your commands we have conferred together for the purpose of considering whether additional means might not at once be devised for preventing, if possible, the recurrence, or at all events diminishing the risk of such and the like accidents in future.

The system of working practised in a district has generally been arrived at after long experience and the trial of different modes, and should not be interfered with except upon clearly different grounds; and as great explosions have occasionally occurred in the neighbourhood of

Barnsley, where in general there appears to be no want of care, and where the special rules are of the most stringent and detailed character, supplying almost every conceivable requirement for safety, we are therefore of opinion that the time has now arrived when it may be fairly questioned whether the system which is there practised might not be modified so as to prevent or mitigate the recurrence of such serious calamities, and whether a limitation of the area of coal to be worked, and of the number of men to be at one time employed in a mine working with one pair of pit shafts, would tend towards the same desirable result.

As to the "Talk-o'-th'-Hill" Colliery explosion, upon the authority of Mr. Wynne, it took place, not from any material defect of the provisions of the Act, but because of the first general and several of the special rules, already provided, having been neglected, the general discipline of the mine having been most lax; but the words "under ordinary circumstances" are made the excuse and means of escape from the consequences of neglecting to properly ventilate that part of the mine where the explosion occurred.

In addition to the Arbitration Clause in the Act, a very elastic power is given for providing against the omission of any provision therein by means of special rules under which any matter relating to safety may be provided for and made law, with the same force as if it had been contained in the Act itself, without the interference of Parliament. Under the circumstances therefore, we feel reluctant to propose any alterations in the law which, on the whole, appears to be working well; but as our attention has been especially drawn to the matter, after the most careful deliberation, we beg most respectfully to solicit your attention to the following points, upon each of which a majority of inspectors of mines are of opinion that alterations in, and additions to, the present law, may to some extent tend to lessen the loss of life from accidents in mines; they are as follows:

First General Rule.—The inspectors feel a difficulty in recommending that the words "under ordinary circumstances" be expunged from this rule, however much they may feel to do so, on the ground that extraordinary circumstances, such as sudden outbursts of gas, and other matters over which there is no control, do actually occur.

Third General Rule (Section 10 of 23 & 24 Vict. C. 151).—That the words "required to be" be struck out, and the rule would then read as follows:—

3. Whenever safety lamps are used they shall be first examined and securely locked by a person or persons duly authorised for this purpose

Fifth General Rule.—That the following rule be substituted for No. 5:—

5. Every working and pumping pit or shaft shall be properly fenced at all times excepting when repairs or other operations may require the temporary removal of the fence.

Ninth General Rule.—That the words after "shaft" be struck out, and the rule will then read:—

9. A sufficient cover overhead shall be used when lowering or raising persons in every working pit or shaft.

Thirteenth General Rule.—That after the word "proper," the words "or efficient" be inserted, and the rule will then read thus:—

13. Every steam boiler shall be

provided with a proper or efficient steam gauge, water gauge, and safety-valve.

Fifteenth General Rule—That the following should be substituted for this rule:–

15. Every place likely to contain a dangerous accumulation of gas or water shall be approached by a narrow working place not exceeding 12 feet wide, in which there shall be at least one bore-hole kept constantly in advance, and with flank bores on each side.

That the following new General Rules be added:–

16. In all workings in coal, where safety lamps are used as the means of lighting, no blasting powder shall be used in such a mine.

17. All working pits, where steam or water power is used for winding shall be fitted with a guide.

13th Section.—This clause appears to be one-sided, and it is desirable, if with due regard to the rights of all parties concerned, that the ordinary mode of arbitration should be substituted.

19th Section.—Any accident reported as a "serious accident," but which may ultimately result in

death, must be again reported.

21st Section.—As this section is not quite explicit, it is proposed that "pit shafts of" be added after "the" the fifteenth word from the end of the section; it will then read thus:–

21. Pit shafts of the same to be, and to be kept, securely fenced for the prevention of accidents.

22nd Section,—That where the maximum penalty is £20 the minimum penalty should not be less than £5.

Act 25 & 26 Vict. c. 79: That in addition to the injunction provided for by the sixth section of this Act, there should be a penalty of £5 per day for every day during which the offence continues after notice thereof has been given.

The inspectors are of the opinion that the present number of 12 inspectors is sufficient for carrying out the Act as it now exists. It is not contemplated that they should act as viewers or managers of collieries, but that they should be in the districts, that matters may be referred to them; and that upon accidents occurring which may appear to be of a nature to require it, or upon removable danger being reported to them, or their having reason to suspect danger, inspections may be made, and the requisite steps taken to enforce the provisions of the law. Such investigations press the responsibility of the management upon the only parties to whom it attaches, and produce good effect by causing precautions to be taken which are likely to prevent a recurrence of accidents. If the view taken by some persons, that inspection should reach further than this, were acted upon, it would tend to relieve the owners and managers of mines of the responsibility which now devolves upon them, and to throw it upon the Government, which, unless the inspectors were made as numerous as the managers and had an equally numerous staff, with power of control over the expenditure, they could not possibly undertake. The ventilation of coal mines requires hourly supervision, and, notwithstanding all the care and attention that can be bestowed, serious accidents will, we fear, occasionally occur. The responsibility must rest somewhere; and if it is intended to place it upon the Government, then the whole subject will require reconsideration.

I have, &c,

(signed) *James P. Baker.*

The Right Hon.
S. H. Walpole MP

MINUTES OF EVIDENCE TAKEN
BEFORE THE
SELECT COMMITTEE ON MINES

THOMAS WYNNE Esq., called
in, and Examined

691 *Chairman.* YOU are the Government Inspector of the district, which includes the Talke-o'-th'-Hill Colliery?—I am. What district do you call it?—The North Stafford, Shropshire, and Cheshire district.

692 You attended, did you not, the inquest which was held on some victims of that explosion?—I did; I attended the whole of the meetings.

693 Going through the list of the jury, speaking now merely as to the composition of the jury, are you in a condition to say whence they came from, and what they were?—Nearly all of them were from the neighbourhood.

694 The Rev. Mr McHutchin, the foreman; who was he?—He was the vicar of the parish.

695 Then there was James Dickinson, of Clayton; what was

he?—Clayton is some distance; about seven miles away: and he is a large farmer; I think he used to be a draper.

696 Had he nothing to do with mines?—He is part owner in a colliery.

697 Thomas Emberton, of Tunstall; do you know anything of him?—He keeps a shop in Tunstall; that is a portion of the Potteries, five or six miles away.

698 Is he mixed up with coal owners or colliers in any way?—Not at all; he had a small colliery some seven or eight years ago, but he is not now connected with any colliery.

699 He had been connected with a colliery of his own, had he?—Yes

700 Henry Gillard, of Tunstall, what is he?—I think he is agent for the Duke of Bridgewater's Canal Carrying Company.

701 What they chiefly carry is coal, is it not?—No, not at all.

702 John Betley, of Audley; do you know anything of him?—I do not; I think he is a farmer.

703 How far is Audley from the place of the inquest?—About three miles.

704 Richard Read (Rhead *sic*), of Talke Pits; what is he?—That is close to the place. He is a labourer.

705 Daniel Johnson, New Road,; what is he?—I think he is a farmer, as far as my knowledge goes.

706 John Turnock, Talke Pits; what would he be?—A pensioner.

707 John Daniels, of Red Street; do you know anything of him? I think he is a collier but I am not sure.

708 Thomas Sherman, of Butt Lane; do you know of him?—A collier.

709 Henshall Moss, of Red Street; who is he?—He is connected with a small ironstone colliery as owner, and brick manufacturer.

710 Ralph Hilditch, Kidsgrove; what is he?—I think he is an auctioneer and valuer.

711 George Shenton, of Alsager?—I do not know what he is , but think a schoolmaster.

712 Elijah Corbett, of Talke, who is he?—I believe he is a publican, as far as my memory goes, but I would not speak positively.

713 Will you tell us generally whether you are satisfied with the manner in which that inquiry was conducted?—It is hardly fair to reflect upon the jury. There were some little things that were not satisfactory.

714 Do you think that the

demeanour of the jury was likely to convey an impression of distrust to the workmen?—One or two things that were done might have conveyed that impression, but the coroner, I thought, immediately put that right.

715 You had no fault to find with the conduct and demeanour of the coroner?—No; he is one of the ablest coroners I ever met, and the most pains-taking.

716 Is it your view that you are responsible for this report of the proceedings?—It is.

717 Where did you get this report of the proceedings which has been presented to Parliament?—I got it from the reporter to the Stafford county paper.

718 You did not employ any reporter?—I did not. I named it to Mr. Cherry to be very careful in taking his report, as it would be very useful to me in reporting to the Home Office.

719 You would probably not be authorised to employ a reporter without the consent of the Home Office?—I should not.

720 Should you have obtained their consent if you had asked for it?—I have no doubt that I should, but our county paper is conducted on those principles that I could perfectly depend upon the report whenever they sent their chief reporter.

721 It appears from this report that on one occasion when Mr. Coe, who was examined on behalf of the management, said that a great deal of credit was due to Mr. Johnson (Manager. *sic.*) and Mr. N i c h o l l s, (*Under Manager Overseer. sic*) and the jury expressed their approval of this sentiment by stamping on the floor; was that correct?—There was something of that kind.

722 Were you present when that was done?—I was

723 When you say that there was something of that kind, was that distinctly done?—It was.

724 Did the act of stamping seem to be general among the jury?—That I could not say; we have not the proper conveniences at all times; sometimes the people are standing close up to the jury, and there is not the separation that there is in a court of justice between the jury and the audience.

725 I do not see it stated in that report that the coroner interfered to reprove the jury for that expression of feeling; do you remember whether he did interfere or not?—I consider that the reproof which he gave by his looks, was as severe a reproof as I

ever saw administered.

726 You mean that when the jury stamped their feet, the coroner looked hard at them?—He did.

727 But he did not say anything to them?—No, it passed away without anything being said.

728 With regard to the persons of whom it is said great credit is due; who were Mr. Johnson and Mr. Nicholls; you had not thought that any great credit was due to them?—No; as the committee will see by the questions which I put I did not think that any great credit was due to them.

729 Had you not very plainly intimated by your evidence that you thought considerable blame attached to Mr. Johnson and Mr. Nicholls?—Yes and that is my opinion still.

730 That is not only your opinion, but by the part which you had taken in the inquiry, you had plainly shown that you did not approve of Mr. Johnson and Mr. Nicholls?— I had.

731 And Mr. Evans had also intimated the same, had he not?—I think that he had not cross-examined any witness up to that time; I think he cross-examined Mr. Coe.

732 Do you remember that in the early part of the inquiry Mr.

Johnson had said that the responsibility for the underground works rested with Mr. Nicholls?—He did.

733 Do you assent with that view of Mr. Johnson's duties?—I did not.

734 This is Mr. Johnson's statement at page 15 of the report; "As far as the general management is concerned, I am not held responsible for what is done in the pit, beyond the sinking of the shafts"?—Yes; that is his view.

735 And that was the view the jury took, but you do not concur?—I do not.

736 Looking at the condition of the mine as it was disclosed by the evidence, do you think that the accident might have been prevented by inspection?—No, I do not think that inspection would have prevented the accident; it was the want of knowledge on the part of the managers.

737 Assuming it to have arisen from the want of knowledge on the part of the manager, is not that just one of the points which would have been apparent to a good inspector, and which he would have been able to notice?—That is, supposing the inspector had been there a week before.

738 You do not consider that the

accident was owing to something in the general management of the mine, but to an error which had recently been committed?—In my opinion it was continuing the levels on, when they had no means of ventilating them, that caused the accident.

739 And that it did not arise from any defect in the general management?—No, the explosion did not arise from that.

740 It arose from a want of general skill in the manager, but not from any defect in the general management?—It did.

741 The particular defect to which you attribute the explosion would not have been apparent to an inspector, if he had visited the mine a month before, or two months before?—I do not think that it was in anything like the same state two months before.

742 Therefore, unless the inspection had been very frequent indeed, it would not have prevented the accident?—No, it would not.

743 Or unless the inspector had happened to have gone there a week before?—Certainly.

744 If it were a rule that the inspector was to visit the mine once a year, or twice a year, or even three times a year, do you think that that might not have had any effect in preventing this accident?—No; because the cause of the accident in my opinion had been produced within the last month or so, by driving levels without any means of ventilation.

745 When had you last been at the mine?—Just a twelvemonth before, within a day or two.

746 Did you make any observations at that time?—They had then not opened more than half the work that there is now, and none had been opened at the part where the explosion took place.

747 Had you made any observations upon the management of the mine?—No. What portion was then opened was very well ventilated indeed; and, indeed, at the time of the explosion there was plenty of air in the pit; but it was not made that use of that ought to have been made.

748 There was a good supply of air, but they did not take pains for its circulation?—That was exactly the case.

749 At the time of the explosion, was the defect in the jig one of the causes which interfered with the circulation of the air; was it that the door got propped open by the

train?—Yes, that was the immediate cause.

750 And the train getting off the rail, could not be moved for some time?—Yes, that was so.

751 And until the train could be moved the door could not be shut?—Yes, it could not.

752 Was that the state of things existing when you visited the mine a year before?—That portion of the work was not then driven; it was part full of water.

753 If you had noticed it; that was a point, was it not, to which you should have called the the attention of the manager?—Yes; in fact I was astonished that any practical manager should attempt to carry on work in that way.

754 You think that that accident was owing to bad management?—Entirely.

755 That is to say, to the want of skill and knowledge in the manager?—It was.

756 Does that suggest to you the expediency of taking other means than are now taken by the law to provide for the knowledge and efficiency of the managers?—I do not see any practical solution to that difficulty; I find that in every case where I have induced them to get a good manager the accidents immediately decrease.

757 What is your test of a good manager?—He should be a man who thoroughly understands the working of mines, and should be of that class that he can command others to do the duties that belong to subordinates.

758 Before you recommend a man as a proper and good manager, how do you test his ability?—If I am asked whether I think such a man is competent for a particular post, my test is that I have known that he has had the management of a large colliery, and has conducted it well.

759 But before he was put into the management of a large colliery, how could his fitness have been ascertained?—By having served the proper time under a proper mining engineer, and having been placed somewhere where he had the practical management of a mine under the supervision of another person.

760 Having subjected his fitness to all those tests, in your own mind you would be able to give him a certificate, would you not?—Yes.

761 But supposing you were on a board having to give a certificate to a manager, should you feel any great difficulty in testing his

fitness either by examination or by testimonials?—I do not think that an inspector is the proper person to place the person whom he has to supervise. It would be very hard for an inspector toto place a manager at a colliery, and then have to turn round on him and say you are a bad manager.

762 You think it would give an inspector an interest in rather screening those whom he recommended?—I think that inspectors are not parties to perform that duty. I would rather put it the other way; that each colliery owner should employ a manager who is satisfactory to the inspector.

763 Therefore you would give the inspector some control over the appointment of the manager? —The black spot of my district is, undoubtedly, the want of good managers.

764 And the inspector has no power of disallowing the appointment of the men?—No.

765 Do you think it would be a good thing that the appointment of a manager should be subject to the approval of the inspector of the district?—I think it would have a very good effect if the inspector could say to the owner, I think you must take the responsibility

yourself, unless you get a better manager.

766 Do you think it would have a good effect upon the management of mines if the manager were liable to lose his certificate or to have it suspended?—At the present time the punishment is very great, as managers very often lose their situation if anything serious happens.

767 But sometimes they do not?—No; it is so in some cases.

768 Has either Mr. Nicholls or Mr. Johnson lost his situation?— They have appointed a consulting engineer to take charge of the mine; he is a gentleman who gave evidence on occasion; a Mr. Rigby, a very able man.

769 You mean that they have been put down in a lower position than they formerly occupied? —Yes; but not Mr. Johnson; Mr. Johnson does not now take the responsibility underground at all.

770 The coroner, in his charge, rather goes out of his way, does he not, to commend Mr. Johnson and Mr. Nicholls?—Not Mr. Nicholls, I think.

771 The coroner states this at page 38 of the Report: "But if the jury could point out any particular in which an improvement could be made in the management of the

colliery, he was convinced, from the knowledge of the parties, that Mr. Johnson and Mr. Nicholls would pay the best attention to their recommendations?"—Yes he said that; and I think so too.

772 Those are words of commendation are they not?—No. That is only with regard to the future he did not commend the management; he took a different view, perhaps, to what I did as to Mr. Johnson's position, but not as to Mr. Nicholls.

773 But neither of them has lost his situation?—No, but there is a gentleman put in between the two.

774 Over Mr. Nicholls?—Yes.

775 Have any actions, that you know of, been brought against Mr. Nicholls by the widows and children of those who were killed?—Not that I am aware of.

776 The accident, in great measure, was due to the carelessness of the men, was it not?—That is too often the case.

777 I mean in this particular case?—I think not; the fault lay with the manager.

778 But did it not appear that there had been great carelessness on the part of the men, and very inefficient control over them?—Yes, but then I do not see it in that light, that the men are to be so blamed as they often are for doing what is wrong, when those who are put in authority over them see it daily and wink at it.

779 Apart from the difficulty and danger that had arisen within a month of the explosion, there was previous to that a general want of discipline in this mine, was there not?—Nothing could be worse than the discipline.

780 How was it that that was not apparent to you when you visited the mine?—I could not tell whether the men had got lamp-keys in their pockets if I had visited every week, or whether they smoked. As you will see, I make a recommendation that the law shall authorise the manager or banksman to search the men; there is no authority now to search them.

781 Was not one of the charges against the management of the mine, that locks of the lamps were very insufficient?—It was not fair to put it so; they were only insufficient through the constant using of bad tools to lock and unlock them.

782 You mean that the locks had been spoilt by being perpetually tampered with?—Yes.

783 Did you satisfy yourself in that respect, or is it your practice

when you inspect mines to satisfy yourself that the lamps are in a proper state?—Nearly every lamp I come to I take in my hand and give a twist to see if it is locked.

784 Of course you did not smell any tobacco when you inspected the mine?—No, I did not.

785 Was there nothing in your inspection of the mine the year before to indicate that the discipline of the mine was very lax?—No; they were only driving what is called straight work, that is the levels and the headings; there was no goaf created.

786 You state, do you not, that there was plenty of air in the pit when you went there?—Yes, apparently.

787 Was there plenty of air in the most distant workings?—There was, as far as it was opened then, and there was in December last plenty of air down the pit. If the explosion had not taken place that day, the next day it would not have taken place. They were so near cutting through, that when it was tested, it was only a yard through.

788 Another yard would have made a current of air?—It would.

789 Was there not something in the state of the atmosphere which tended to cause the explosion?—Yes there was; but what I blamed them for was their persistence in getting coals before they had got the air; if they had delayed driving those forward heads until this yard was cut through, there would have been no danger in their working.

790 With regard to your general opinion of the conduct of the jury on that occasion, was it such as to gain the confidence of the workmen?—After that expression, I saw every desire to hear everything that could be offered to them in evidence for or against the management.

791 Have you any suggestion to offer as to the composition of the jury?—No.

792 The jury, from your description, was composed pretty equally of different classes of persons, was it not?—Yes.

793 There was no preponderance of what I may call the owner's interest upon that jury, in your opinion?—No I do not think there was.

794 They were farmers and tradesmen and workmen and miners themselves, and likewise owners?—Yes and some practical colliers.

795 Did it appear to you at the time that the composition of the

jury might have been improved in any way?—No I do not think that it could very well; but Mr. Johnson is a man who stands very high as a man, and perhaps when they heard that he was likely to be inculpated by the witnesses, they felt pleased that they should have an opportunity of exculpating him from any charge.

796 Then the impression which that very improper ebullition of feeling made upon your mind was, that Mr. Johnson was a very popular person and that anything that tended to exculpate him excited an amount of public sympathy, and they expressed it in that improper way?—Yes; as I thought in a very unseemly way.[*]

797 Are you able to say whether any of the working colliers themselves joined in that expression of feeling?—I could not say; but for the first day or two there was great difficulty in getting any of the working colliers to say anything against the working of the mine; as we progressed, we found things come out which we could not possibly get out in the first day or two

798 Then your impression of the

---

[*] This was when the jury had stamped their feet.

proceedings at first, at any rate, was that there was a desire if possible, to shield Mr. Johnson? There is no question about it, that there was such a desire among the workmen themselves; but as we progressed the thing naturally developed itself and we could see where all the fault lay.

799 And the coroner used his authority to enforce discipline upon the jury, in fact?—Yes; and I was very glad that he did.

800 The ultimate cause of the accident was the exposing of a naked light, which exploded the gas, was it not?—Yes; it was.

801 And that gas ought not to have been there, had the ventilation been efficient?—No, it would not have been there under proper management.

802 Is not the exposure of a naked light, in other parts of that mine which are well ventilated, an extremely dangerous experiment?—It was then.

803 A naked light is forbidden in the mine is it not?—It is, except just in the main road; in the intake of air.

804 You state, in the first place, that in your opinion the explosion was caused by an error in management, by a defective system of ventilation in that

particular part of the mine, but that no ulterior proceedings have been taken in the shape of actions against the manager?—Not that I am aware of; I have not heard of anything of the kind.*

805 May not the fact be explained by the circumstances of the ultimate cause of the explosion having been carelessness on the part of the men?—I think it would be more owing to the immense kindness that was displayed by Mr. Johnson and Mr. Smith-Child, and all the parties interested, towards the widows and orphans.

806 Then the fact of those proceedings not having been taken is really a matter which reflects great credit upon the widows and the connections of those unfortunate men?—Very great credit; it is in consequence of what has been done for them with so ungrudging a hand.

[Paragraphs 808 to 860 not shown]

THOMAS EVANS, Esq., called in; and Examined

861 *Chairman.* YOU are an Inspector of Mines in Derbyshire are you not?—Yes, for the

* Meaning here legal actions by the families of the deceased

Midland Counties.

862 And you were directed by the Government to attend the inquest at Talke-o'-th'-Hill, as well as Mr. Wynne, were you not?—I did attend the inquest with Mr. Wynne.

863 By the direction of the Home Office, did you not?—I think Mr. Wynne did consult Mr. Walpole.

864 Have you heard what Mr. Wynne stated with regard to that inquest?—Yes.

865 Do you agree with what he stated?—Generally I do.

866 Is there any point on which you do not agree with him?—I think the cause of that explosion arose from the want of discipline, the want of system, and bad management.

867 Do you think that it arose from causes which might have been prevented by more frequent inspection?—No, I think not.

868 Unless the inspection had happened to have been very close before the accident?—Even if it had been close before, I scarcely think it would, because small matters of detail which no inspector could possibly see by inspection, continuing daily getting from bad to worse, and I think that that may itself have caused the explosion.

869 What are the little matters of detail which an inspector could not see?—For instance, an inspector could not detect the constant opening of safety lamps, smoking and firing shots in the presence of gas, he could not tell whether the fireman examined the workings before the shots were fired, and all those little matters of detail, any one of which might have caused the explosion.

870 Those things must depend, must they not, on the efficiency and judgement of the underground manager?—No doubt.

871 Will not an experienced inspector be able generally to form a correct opinion as to the efficiency of a manager without entering into those details?—Yes; generally he could.

872 Do not you think that there was something in the management of that mine, apart from those little details which would escape the eye, which would have shown to an experienced inspector that the management was not good?—If he had been there perhaps a day or two before the explosion he would of course have seen that ventilation was very insufficient in the lower workings.

873 But that is only in case he had been there very shortly

before?—It is a new colliery, and there is no extent of workings: they are practically just opening out, and according to the evidence, and I believe it to be correct, they have 25,000 cubic feet of air in the pit, and if they had only taken pains the air conducted to the face of the workings, the pit might have easily been kept safe.

[Paragraphs 874 to 883 not shown]

---

884 Was your opinion favourable as to the demeanour and conduct of the jury on the occasion of the Talke-o'-th'-Hill inquiry?—I think so generally; the expression of feeling at one part of the inquiry was not proper in my opinion but I think that arose chiefly in this way; at the commencement of the inquiry the evidence produced was brought forward by the owners themselves, merely explaining the best part of the colliery; that is to say presenting their side of the question, and that evidence met with the approbation of some of the jury, but when they heard the other side of the case brought out by Mr. Wynne and myself, I think they altered their opinion and took the correct view of it.

148

885 But at the time that the jury made manifestation of their opinions, they had already heard, had they not, what Mr. Wynne's opinion was?—No, I think not; at least they had not heard his evidence. Mr. Wynne was examined on the last day but one of the inquiry.

886   Do you not conceive that Mr. Wynne, by his examination of the previous witnesses, had plainly shown that he was not satisfied with the management of the colliery?—I really do not remember; I know that Mr. Coe was a witness brought forward by the colliery owners themselves, and that he had not been cross-examined when that exhibition of feeling took place.

[Paragraphs 887 to 916 not shown]

917 Mr. Wynne has described the cause of the accident at the Talke-o'-th'-Hill Colliery, and stated that unless he had happened to have examined it about a week or so before the accident occurred, his examination would have been of no use to have prevented the accident; but mismanagement of that description would be very frequent in an older colliery,

supposing mismanagement to exist, would it not?—Yes, in little matters of detail: for instance, supposing the extreme end of the level was fiery, unless the air is kept directly up to the face it would fill with gas.

918 So that if there were anything like systematic neglect or want of precaution, the inspector would discover it, would he not?—If he went into every hole in the colliery he might see it.

919 Supposing there were systematic neglect to carry adequate ventilation into all those new headings, is that a matter which your personal visit to a colliery would enable you to discover, even if your attention had not been specially called to it by a complaint on the part of the colliers?—No, not in all cases.

920 It would be no part of your duty to go into the new headings and see whether proper provision was made for ventilation?—Yes it might be a part of my duty, if I thought that anything was wrong: but if you take a large colliery, there may be 60 or 70 miles of roads underground, and it is quite impossible to examine them all.

921 It is quite impossible to examine the whole, but do not you when you examine a colliery lay

down for yourself certain rules to guide your examination, in order to test the efficiency of the precautions taken by the manager?—Yes.

922 Would not the visiting of those headings or at any rate a heading here and there, be one of the steps which you would take?—I should do that, but it would not ensure the perfect ventilation of all the headings by going into only two or three of them.

923 But it would enable you in the long run to discover whether in this particular instance the management was or was not careful, would it not?—No, I do not think it would. In the case of the Talke-o'-th'-Hill Colliery, three weeks before the explosion the colliery might have been perfectly free from gas.

[Paragraphs 924 to 933 not shown]

934——[Mr. Powell.] In speaking of the Talke-o'-th'-Hill Colliery as being one of small extent do you mean that the existing works are limited in proportion, or that the entire colliery when opened out will be small in extent?—I do not know what the acreage of the colliery may be. I am talking of the present condition of the workings; at least of their condition at the time of the accident.

935 But are the workings laid out with a view to getting the coal from a very considerable area?—I do not know at all what the area might be but I mean to say this, that the shafts have only just been sunk, and that the workings are comparatively limited in extent What they may eventually become I do not know.

936 But would not the size of the shafts and the whole appearance of the arrangements bear some relation to the extent of the field?—No the shafts are a good size; I think they are 12 feet.

937 And the field is a good deal traversed with faults, I understand?—I do not know that country.

Author's note.

These extracts are presented in like format to the original Parliamentary documents printed at the time (1867). They reflect the severity of the pit disasters at Barnsley and at Talke-o'-th'-Hill and this report to the Secretary of State was thought to be instrumental in setting in train the future requirement for technical certification of managers and surveyors in the mines.

As I read and researched the documents, the' Reminiscence' itself, the newspaper reports of the disasters and the inquests and the record of the Mining Inspectors' reports to the Home Office, I was deeply impressed by the quality and usage of the written English. The vocabulary throughout is precise and eloquent. There is no ambiguity and I did not encounter a single typographical error. The written word was really the only vehicle for bringing information into the public domain and creating a lasting record of important events. Mr Wynne, the Government Inspector of Mines, when questioned, said that he did not appoint an official recorder at the inquest because he knew that the reporter from the local newspaper could be relied upon to do a first class job and could not be bettered. What a tribute to the professional and conscientious approach of men who took such pride in their work. I doubt the same could be said today. It is the beautiful quality of the language that, for me, makes this account so compelling and moving.

CHAPTER ELEVEN

'THE WINDS OF CHANGE'

'I'm making the ladies and gentlemen warm
Though I ain't got no Latin or learning
I get them their coals for winter and storm
But they don't think of me while they're burning'.

From:-'*A Reminiscence of a Collier's Life*'
Charles Lawton, (1839 –1921)

George Orwell, (1903 – 1950) wrote in his documentary 'The Road to Wigan Pier' (1937), the following.

"In a way it is humiliating to see coal miners working. It raises up in you momentary doubts about your own status as an intellectual and a superior person. All of us owe the comparative decency of our lives to the poor drudges underground, blackened to the eyes, with their throats full of coal dust driving their shovels forward with arms and belly muscles of steel".

A LITTLE HISTORY

In the first half of the 19th century the mining industry slumbered in the doldrums. There was complacency, an acceptance by all concerned that the conditions prevailing underground were tolerable, that accidents were an unavoidable and inevitable part of extracting coal from the earth. Bad practices of previous generations prevailed. The full potential of coal as the driving force of the nation had yet to be recognised. All this was to be changed radically and violently as the industrial revolution gathered pace. In 1856 about 1.3 million tons of coal was extracted per year, by 1870 the figure had risen to 4 million tons. The changes would benefit the miners in the long run, but in the short term much hardship and loss of life had to be endured.

The iron and steel industry was burgeoning, as were the Potteries. Foundries were very active from 1840 onwards. Names like Sneyd, Kinnersley and Heath all had interests in both ironstone and coal mining and they amassed great wealth. Robert Heath was reputed to be the greatest private ironmaster in Britain. Steam was the motive power for ships and trains. Cobwebs of railway track criss-crossed the country and these, along with the canals, facilitated the transporting of coal from coast to coast with speed and efficiency. Sea-borne trade was overtaken by rail in 1867. The demand for coal was insatiable and big profits were to be made above ground. However, underground there was a different story and a heavy price to pay. As Charles Lawton says, in his 'Reminiscences', the constant cry from the proprietors of the mines was, 'Get out more coal.' The incentive to the workers was not better pay for their efforts but rather sanctions if targets were not met. There's nothing 'new ' about Tony Blair's New Labour then!

In their efforts to satisfy the demands of the bosses the underlooker turned a blind eye as safety procedures were circumvented. Often men openly smoked tobacco underground, taking matches into their workplace or tampering with their lamps to light their pipes. In order to speed up the process of extracting the coal the whole method of working had been changed from 'wedging', which was comparatively safe, to blasting, which was definitely a high risk operation. The rules, which every collier was supposed to read and understand, clearly stated that no smoking materials were allowed underground. Dynamite was only to be made available to the qualified 'shot firer' in small amounts at a time. We read in the Mine Inspectors' reports time after time that there was a virtual powder shop at the pit bottom. Often it was the case that the shot firer was not available when he was needed so, rather than waste precious time and risk being short on his day's output, the collier would get dynamite from the underlooker and fire the shot himself, often with disastrous results. In the years 1866 to 1870 there were 461 deaths in Staffordshire due to explosions.

'The Winds Of Change'

We have to remember that, until 1842 the workforce underground was not entirely male. Mature women and children, boys and girls as young as ten and adolescents were also toiling, half-naked in the oppressive heat of the pit. Many women and girls were subjected to abuse of all sorts, when standards of decency and morality gave way to bestiality and depravity. These were facts of their poor lives. In 1840 a Children's Employment Commission was set up to investigate the 'mental and moral' conditions experienced by children working underground. Parliament, after considering the recommendations of the inspectors, introduced the Mines Act of 1842 heralding the end of the hated 'butty' system and enforcing a regime of much stricter control. It was no longer acceptable for any females to be employed underground although they still carried out heavy menial tasks at the pit bank. Boys under the age of ten were not allowed to be at the pit at all. This regulation was often breached especially where seams were thin. Managers had to gain a certificate of competency before they could undertake their duties and, once in post, they were responsible for everything that happened underground. More Mines Inspectors were appointed and they were more assiduous in their inspections being required to report to the Home Office on every mine in their area on a regular basis. These new regulations certainly brought great improvements but miners were a law unto themselves and many disasters, wholly avoidable occurred in the early 1870s to be recorded as 'accidents' although in reality the root causes were carelessness and wanton disregard for safety rules.

CHAPTER TWELVE

STAFFORDSHIRE SENTINEL 22ND FEBRUARY, 1873

TERRIBLE COLLIERY EXPLOSION AT TALKE-ON-THE-HILL

The colliery and the pit of the North Staffordshire Coal and Iron Company, Talke-on-the-Hill, where, on the 13th of December, 1866, by a terrible explosion, some ninety bodies underground were in a moment struck dead, was, on Tuesday the scene of another frightful catastrophe. Towards 9 a.m., as the men were at work, an explosion of gas took place in the 8ft. seam and every man in the working was killed. Tidings of the horrible event soon spread around the neighbourhood, and crowds of people, some seeking with frantic eagerness to ascertain the fate of relatives and friends; others attracted by an irresistible impulse made up of sympathy and curiosity; and others anxious to render aid thronged the colliery. The pit bank was a scene of great excitement, but, as soon as possible after the accident, volunteers descended the mine, and attempted an exploration of the shattered workings, coming up again after a time exhausted and unable to give any clear idea as to

the extent of mischief wrought, or the number of the dead. In the absence of reliable information, rumour gave out exaggerated accounts as to the loss of life, it being currently and confidently stated that some thirty or forty had perished. Fortunately this was not so, it being found that but about one half of that number were missing. Every effort was made to reach the source of the explosion, but for some time little progress could be made on account of the state of the pit. From the nature of the coal, a large quantity of dust has at all times to be contended with in the eight-foot seam, and an accumulation of this dust, with a large quantity of bratticing, being set on fire by the explosion, increased the difficulties that had to be overcome; and when the fire was extinguished the after-damp impeded the progress of the workers. The exploration went on all night; the workers continuing nobly at their melancholy task in spite of fatigue and intense cold. The numbers of persons assembled at the pit entrance thinned as the night wore on, and as the small hours grew late and larger few were left besides the police and others on duty. As daylight returned, the bank began to be repeopled, and all the next day crowds gathered round the pit, hundreds of persons coming from different parts of the district; the village was in a state of commotion such as unhappily only visits it on such melancholy occasions such as this. Fourteen bodies were brought from the pit on Wednesday. Twelve were taken to the Swan Inn and two to their homes. The Swan was a centre of attraction, dividing labours with the pit, every room being crowded. The bodies recovered were placed in a large room upstairs, and decently attired in white calico dresses and covered with white sheets. The process of identification went on all day, but some of the bodies were fearfully mutilated, which rendered identification very difficult. One or two were wrongly claimed, but under the careful attention of Mr. Brownell, mining engineer of the company, who, after being hard at work all night at the pit, undertook the duty of waiting in the room, and taking down the names and addresses of the unfortunate men as they were identified, the process went steadily on. Mr. Brownell also gave direction for

the preparation of coffins, the interment of the deceased being undertaken by the company.

On Wednesday afternoon it was ascertained that the number of the dead would not exceed 20, but as several belonged to remote parts of the district, the exact number could not even then be told. For some time three of the bodies could not be identified, so terribly were they mutilated and disfigured and all were fearfully burned. At times so great was the curiosity of the persons who crowded the Inn to see the bodies, that it was with great difficulty the police were able to keep them back and it was next to impossible for those whose duty called them to be there to get in or out. When but one of the bodies remained unknown, numbers of persons crushed towards the steps where the bodies lay and pleaded hard for permission to view the dreadful spectacle to see if they could recognise that one, but the police, with commendable firmness, carried out their instructions to keep the curious away. This in one or two instances unavoidably led to relatives suffering the hardship of being refused admission. During a rush, a poor fellow with face sooty black with the dust of the pit, only where tears had left their tracks down his cheeks, pushed his way through the crowd. Addressing the officer he said, "Let me go upstairs to see if my lad is among them." The officer replied, "I cannot let you go." The poor fellow replied, "You must let me go. This morning they brought the wrong boy home, and since the mistake was found out I have been working in the pit to see if I can find my lad, and now I want to see if he is here; I have only just come up." This prevailed, and the heart-broken father going upstairs turned down the covering from the faces of the dead, now and then gazing intently through his tears to recognise, if possible, in the scorched and disfigured features he beheld, those of his son. The following are the names of the victims of the sad catastrophe.

1 John Birchenough, 35, married, and three children, Acres Nook, Goldenhill.

2 John Stamper, 27, single, Talke.

3 James Hackney, 14, single, Congleton.

4 Benjamin Booth, 21, Single, Talke.

5 Thomas Booth, 41, married, and four children, Talke.

6 Thomas Breeze, 25, married, and three children, Talke

7 Thomas William Harrison, 14, single, Talke.

8 David Winkle, 16, single, Talke.

9 John Shannon, 19, single, Talke.

10 William Jones, 23, single, Talke.

11 Thomas Grocott, 30, married, and one child, Talke.

12 Richard Sherwin, 14, single, Talke.

13 William Lowndes, 20, single, Talke.

14 Robert Walker, 17, single, Borthemsley.

15 John Baynham, 38, married, and three children, Talke.

16 Henry Grocott, 27, married, no children, Talke.

17 Francis Birch, 17, single, Talke.

18 Samuel Kennion, 16, single, Red-street.

Benjamin Booth and Thomas Booth were brothers and Thomas Grocott and Henry Grocott were cousins. The young man Kennion was the son of a collier who was killed by the explosion in this pit in December 1866. Lowndes and Sherwin were the men taken to

Gravestone – Frank Birchall, aged 15 years 8 months

Gravestone – Richard Sherwin, aged 13 years

158

their homes. Grocott, Sherwin and Breeze are stated to have been Good Templars and very steady and industrious. Grocott had only been married about a year, and his poor wife had been but a fortnight confined.

The effects of the explosion in the eight-foot seam were very severe, and show that a very large body of gas had broken loose and was fired. The presence of the gas is still unexplained. The fireman (Edwin Durber) who examined the pit on Tuesday morning, reported it to be perfectly safe, and several men who have been spoken to express every confidence in the fireman who fired the shot, stating that he was a most careful man, and would take every precaution before firing the shot. Whether their confidence was justified in this particular instance we shall never know for every one in the working has gone, and the mystery will remain unsolved to the end of time, unless the intensive inspection yet to be made should reveal the secret. One thing is clear, that there was a large bed of gas fired, but how the accumulation came about seems to be beyond human knowledge, at least at present. The general testimony of men employed in the

pit is that the ventilation has been remarkably good and that it has been regarded "safe" to work in. Volunteers from the mining engineers of the district hastened to give their assistance, and rendered valuable aid in the exploration of the pit. Among them were Messrs. R. and W. Oswald, managers of Woodshutts and Harecastle collieries; Mr. Robson Moffatt, manager of Manway colliery; Mr. J. McNay, manager of Smallthorne Colliery; Mr. Foster of Hanley; Mr. Strick jnr. of Hanley; Mr. C. Shute, consulting engineer of the North Staffordshire Coal and Iron Company; and Mr. Hunter, resident viewer; and Mr. Rigby, colliery proprietor, have given the benefits of their advice in the movements.

Continuous relays of men have gone down to explore the pit. These, under the direction of the mining engineers named above, have worked nobly, and in fact no effort has been spared by anyone engaged. As may be supposed, their work was most difficult, not only on account of the want of ventilation, but of the obstructions caused by the force of the explosion. In many places the roof fell in, burying a number of men, and the air courses were blown down, filling the roads with debris. The coal dust set on fire by the explosion extended from the brow to the level. Three horses which were in the wagon road, near the shaft, were killed by the after-damp. A few lamps were found. They were all broken by the force of the explosion, and some had been tampered with. The bodies of the fireman who is supposed to have fired the shot, which it is thought caused the explosion, and another collier, were found together in the place to which they had run for safety after firing. Some of the men at the top of the pit say that they heard two explosions, one after the other; and the force of the explosion is ???? ???? ????*(Sic not readable),* and dust blown up the lower shaft of the pit, having been carried a considerable distance before reaching the shaft. The hooker-on and a boy were blown through a pair of air doors, and emerged with slight injuries. The source of the explosion is several hundred yards from the shaft, and at a depth of three hundred yards from the surface.

On Thursday morning the Vicar of Talke, the Rev. M.W. McHutchin, received from the Bishop of Lichfield and Mr. Smith Child Bart. M.P. the following letters, which will, no doubt be read with interest.

Lollard's Towers, Lambeth, London S.W.
19th February 1873.
> *My Dear Mr. McHutchin,*
> *I am shocked to see in the Times of this morning the report of another colliery accident. My mind is still full of the thoughts of Pelsall. Please take soonest opportunity of assuring the widows and orphans of my sympathy with them in their bereavement, and apply the enclosed cheque for their benefit in any way that you think best.*
> *Yours very faithfully,*
> *G.A .Lichfield.*
Mr. M.W. McHutchin –Cheque £5.

Carlton Club, Pall Mall, London, 19th February.
> *My dear Sir, I am very sorry to see by the papers that there has been another horrible accident at Talke. I shall be glad to hear particulars. I asked Mr. Bruce in the House about it, but he knows nothing yet. Did you not tell me, some time back, that some of the leaders of the colliers union had been publicly speaking against the Miners Relief Society and advised the men not to join! I*

should think this accident will bring the matter home to them. I should think there might be something spared from the former's Talke fund as there is the surplus of the Hartley appeal amounting to several hundreds which is available. Mr. M. Heath and Mr. Goddard are the newly appointed trustees of this latter fund, applications should be made to them at once. I think I asked them for the interest for the Relief Association but Mr. Heath seemed to think the fund only should be applied to similar accidents. Your recent case is, therefore, in point. I sent Mr. Heath's letter to Mr. L.T. Stamer. He is at Kings Road, Brighton – I think. Yours truly,

Smith Child.

Apropos of Sir Smith Child letter, I may mention that only 32 of the men (about 700 in number) employed at Talke colliery are members of the North Staffordshire Coal and Ironstone Workers Permanent Relief Fund, and three of these are amongst the killed. Thomas Breeze (who leaves a widow and four children) John Shannon and Richard Sherwin. The widow of Breeze will receive from the fund the sum of £5 for funeral expenses, 4s. per week for the first two years, 3s. per week for the second two years and 3s. per week for each child until it shall attain the age of 14 years. Shannon was a single man and 3s. will be paid by the fund to his relatives, while the parents of Sherwin, a boy, will receive £5. It is hoped that the miners of the district will speedily see the advantages to be gained by themselves in case of injury, and by their relatives if they should unfortunately lose their life in the mine, by becoming members of this fund, the subscription to pay is but trifling.

The inquest on the bodies of 13 men was opened on Thursday morning at the Swan Inn, Talke before John Booth Esq, coroner and a jury comprised of the following gentlemen, Messrs, G.Shenton, foreman, J.Wright, I.Cliffe. J.Colclough, J.Bolton, A.Hambleton, W.Birch, W.Wright, J.Allcock, C.Hil???, A..N.Other, Jason Ward, G.Baker and J.Crompton. Mr. Hugh Birley, M.P., and Mr. Roseby of Lincoln, two of the directors of the company, were present at the enquiry, as were also the Reverend W.M.McHutchin, vicar of Talke, and also Superintendent Langdon. Mr. T.Sherratt, solicitor, appeared to watch the proceedings on behalf of the company and Mr. Welch, solicitor, on behalf of the friends of the deceased and the Amalgamated Association of Miners. The jury having been sworn, the coroner said they were met together to enquire into the deaths of 18 men, 13 of whose bodies they would have to view, and three who had not yet been recovered from the mine. The only information he possessed was that shortly after nine on Tuesday there was an explosion of gas in a pit belonging to the North Staffordshire Coal and Iron Company, being, he believed, the same pit in which 91 men lost their lives by an explosion in December 1866. Though not so terrible in its results as that accident, the loss of life by the present explosion was very great and carried sorrow into a many families. He did not propose to go fully into the enquiry then, as Mr. Wynne, the Government Inspector of Mines, was in London attending a meeting of Inspectors, and he (the coroner) did not know when he would return or be able to make an examination of the pit in which the accident had occurred. Having taken evidence of identification, he would adjourn the inquest

pending Mr. Wynne's investigation and said they could call reasonable evidence as to the cause of the explosion. Mr. Roseby said that a telegram had been received from Mr. Wynne to the effect that he would be at Talke on Friday morning. The jury then viewed the bodies of the 13 men after which Henry Blood, collier, identified the body of John Birchenough, John Graham, deputy fireman, was next called, and stated that he was employed in the pit in which the explosion occurred. He went to work at eight o'clock on Tuesday morning, and on examining the roadways and workings of the 7ft. seam he found them all right and free from gas. He went to the 8ft. seam where the explosion occurred, with other persons. Proceeding along the level he found the body of Breeze, and then another body but he did not know whether it was Baynham or Lowndes. Baynham's lamp was about 20 yards away from him. He also found the dead bodies of Breeze and John Stamper. Witness was then questioned by the coroner and the foreman as to his duties and he stated that he was employed under a person named Halliday and he had to look after the firing of shots and to see that the workings were kept clear. He went to work every morning at eight o' clock but Halliday was there at half past five. The pit was worked by single shaft. By Mr. Welch; Halliday had charge of both the 7ft. and 8ft. seams. Durber, another fireman, had examined the workings of the 8ft. seam and he made entries of his examination in a book kept for the purpose. He did not see the book on the morning of the explosion. — The foreman; "Will that book be produced?" Coroner; "No doubt it will be produced at the adjourned enquiry." The bodies of the following men were then identified by their relatives or friends. James Hackney, Benjamin Booth, Thomas Breeze, Harrison, David Winkle, Thomas Booth, William Jones, Thomas Grocott, Richard Sherwin, William Lowndes, John Baynham and Robert Walker. The latter body was identified by Mary Cotton, his mother, who was very much affected while giving evidence. Edwin Durber, fireman, Butt Lane, stated that he was employed in the pit in which the accident had happened. He was fireman in the 7ft. and 8ft. seams and it was his practice to examine the roadways and workings of the 7ft. seam and

then make a similar examination of the 8ft. seam, after which he returned to the bottom of the pit to tell his superior, Halliday, the state of the places. He was in the pit on Tuesday morning having descended about half past two o' clock. With a lamp he examined the whole of the 7ft. working places. They were alright and free from gas. He then went into the 8ft. seam and found all right there. He carefully examined the whole of the working places and the roadways and there was not the slightest trace of gas in any of them. He was quite sure that the seams were free from gas. He tried the drift 'gobs' all along the headside but perceived no gas. He then returned to the bottom of the pit, which he reached about five o' clock. At half past five Halliday came down, and he (fireman) told him that all was right and both seams were free from gas. He was 25 years of age and had been a fireman since the 5th of January.

He had worked in a pit since he was 10 years of age, but never before January had any experience as a fireman. He made an entry of the result of his examination of the seams in a book kept for the purpose as soon as he got to the pit bottom. The entry was made before he saw Halliday, and was, as far as he could recollect, in the following terms, "I examined the whole of the places in the 7ft. and 8ft. seams and found them all right." At eight o' clock he was relieved in the 7ft. seam by Graham. Until that time he was engaged firing shots and looking through the workings. He never perceived any gas. He fired three or four shots in the 7ft. workings. The powder used for firing shots was in cartridges and fuses, and the fuse was fired with a wire through a lamp. The lamps were of gauze and the tops were not taken off as it was against orders to do so. In the 8ft. seam he was relieved at half past ten by Thomas Breeze, and he then left the pit. The first thing Breeze would have to do would be to look after the turns, the bratticing, and the firing of shots, but he did not know whether he discharged his duty in that respect. He did not know how many men there were at work in the seam. When he first saw Breeze he told him that the places were all right. He had only seen gas in the pit about twice since he had been fireman. Every day that he was at work he registered the state of the mine in the book at the pit bottom, and

when he was not there it was done by someone else. When he was not at work the night-man, or doggy, generally took his place. If he had made an incorrect register it would have been discovered by the next man who came on duty. There had never been a complaint made against him of making incorrect entries but he had once been reported for not making an entry in a book on the pit bank as well as the one down below ground. *By Mr. Welch;* There was a thirling to the back dip of the 8ft seam. It was being thirled into the seaming or level above, where a man was at work on the day before the explosion. When he examined that thirling there was a little air passing up it, sufficient to keep the place clear. The place was quite clear of gas. *By the coroner;* He knew the deceased, Birchenough, but could not say whether he had any right to carry a lamp key. At this stage the enquiry was adjourned for two hours, there being a report of the finding of another body in the interval. The enquiry was resumed shortly before four, when the body of Henry Grocott (27) had been recovered. The body was in a frightfully mutilated state, and scarcely recognisable. It had been found buried beneath a great lump of rock, near the top end of the workings. The enquiry was adjourned *sine dei.*

The body of Thomas Birch was recovered on Thursday night, and efforts are now being made to discover the burying place of Kennion, whose body may be found at any moment. Grocott, Jones, Breeze and Winkle were buried yesterday afternoon at Talke, some others will be buried today. Mr. Wynne (Government Inspector), has been down, but has not finished his inspection of the pit. Grocott and Breeze were Good Templars and were followed by members of their lodge in regalia. There was a large crowd of people at the entrance to the church. Rev. M.W. McHutchin officiated.

Very solemn service.

Talke Colliery – shaft and cage

Talke Colliery disaster 1873

CHAPTER THIRTEEN

STAFFORDSHIRE ADVERTISER 22ND FEBRUARY 1873

SERIOUS COLLIERY
EXPLOSION AT TALK-O'-TH'-
HILL

EIGHTEEN LIVES LOST

We regret to have to record the particulars of another frightful explosion at the No.1 pit, belonging to the North Staffordshire Coal and Iron Company, at Talk-o'-th'-Hill where, a little more than six years ago, upwards of eighty lives were lost in one day. The township of Talke, in the parish of Audley, is a somewhat ancient village, about three miles from Tunstall, and four from Newcastle-under-Lyme. Talke was chartered for a market in the reign of Henry the Third, but was subsequently neglected, and lost its market. Latterly it has had new life infused into it, and may now be ranked as a busy colliery village.

The colliery in question is to the right of the road leading from the centre of the village to Newcastle, and is worked by a company formed about eight years ago, and re-constituted a few weeks since. The melancholy particulars of the catastrophe of

December 1866, which occurred in the seven foot seam, have not faded from the memory of a large number of the residents of North Staffordshire, and the unfortunate occurrence in an adjoining seam, which we now have to chronicle, though causing less than a fourth of the loss previously occasioned, has awakened a profound feeling of regret that such accidents seem to be unavoidable. There are two main shafts to the pit, a short distance from each other, and on the North of them are two seams of coal being worked – namely the seven foot and the eight foot Banbury coal. The shafts are sunk to a depth of about 350 yards, and the workings of the Banbury coal extend for several hundred yards in the direction of the village. On Tuesday morning a large number of boys and men, probably nearly two hundred, descended the pit to pursue their ordinary calling, and they continued to work till about half-past one in the afternoon. The Banbury coal is said to be a dangerous coal to work; but the pit has every appliance for proper ventilation and on Tuesday morning the whole of the workings were examined by firemen, and reported to be entirely free from gas before the men commenced operations. Some shots were fired in the morning in the eight-foot seam and there was nothing to indicate that it was unsafe to continue work, or even to fire more shots. It is believed that another shot was fired at 1.30. From this, or some other cause – probably the real cause will never be known with absolute certainty – a terrific explosion took place. This was nearly under the principal part of the village, and notwithstanding there was a great distance between the immediate vicinity of the explosion and the main shafts, the sad occurrence was soon made manifest to those on the bank by the report which was heard and the large clouds of dust and smoke which issued to the surface. All the men who were in the various workings who were able to run towards the shaft hurried thither and were as speedily as possible raised to the pit bank. Many poor fellows affected by the after-damp struggled to their utmost to reach the shaft, and, when raised to the surface, were in the greatest agony. Fortunately Dr. Greatorex, Dr. Bruce and Mr. Stephenson, surgeon, were visiting patients at

Talke, and, on learning what had occurred, hastened to the pit bank, and to their praiseworthy and valuable services many of the sufferers owe their recovery from the effects of the dreaded damp. We believe that all who were able to reach the shaft alive have been restored to their usual condition. The medical gentlemen named remained near the pit all the afternoon and night anxious to render any services which might be availing. But, alas! Those who were not soon out of the pit were beyond human aid.

The effects of the explosion were very severe, and it was long before the extent of the damage done could be ascertained. The men and boys in the pit at the time hastened, as we have said, to the shaft, and in doing so most of them left behind them their tools and their lamps. On finding themselves safe many left the bank without reporting themselves; and though no doubt existed that there had been loss of life, the extent of that loss could not be ascertained till the following day. The workings were considerably damaged and some coal dust and bratticing became ignited. The fire was put out with great difficulty, and occasioned some delay in searching the workings for any who might have been left therein. Exploring parties were formed, including Mr. R. Shute, consulting engineer for the North Staffordshire Coal and Iron Company; Mr. Hunter resident viewer; Messrs R. and W. Oswald, managers of Woodshutts and Harecastle collieries; Mr. Robson Moffatt, manager of the Clanway colliery; Mr. J. M'Nay, manager of the Smallthorne colliery, Mr. Foster, of Hanley; and Mr. R.J.Strick of Hanley. Mr. Rigby, colliery proprietor, gave the benefit of his advice in the movements. There were also plenty of willing volunteers among the working colliers, who laboured hard in exploring the damaged workings. Several ineffectual attempts were made to advance from the bottom of the shaft along roadways in the eight-foot seam, the after-damp driving them back to the surface, where, more than once, they had to be placed in the care of the medical gentlemen named above. At length, by raising and lowering the level of water in one of the shafts, ventilation was partially restored, and when the damaged portion of the workings could be approached, dead bodies, sometimes in pairs and sometimes singly, began to be discovered. By Wednesday morning thirteen lifeless bodies were found, and they were removed before daylight to the Swan Inn. In the afternoon another corpse was found, in the evening one more, making fifteen. The sixteenth was found after the inquest had been opened on Thursday. The order in which most of them were found is not known; for, with one or two exceptions, they were not recognisable from their appearance. They were all severely burnt and most of them were sadly mutilated. Two only could be identified on Wednesday morning, – namely William Lowndes, aged 22, and a boy named Richard Sherwin who were removed to the homes of their friends. One body was claimed as being that of Frederick Birch; but on being removed to his father's house and washed, it was discovered that the body was not that of Birch's son. It was returned to the Swan Inn. So shockingly had some been mutilated that it was only by the contents of their pockets or parts of their clothing that they could be identified. Mr. Brownell, the mining engineer of the company (who had been hard at work all night in the pit), and police sergeant Torr, waited in the room on Wednesday for several hours whilst the process of identification was going on, the former taking down the names and addresses of the men as they were identified. Mr. Brownell also gave directions for the preparation of the coffins, the interments of the deceased being undertaken by the company. There was an uncertainty, on Wednesday, as to the actual number in the pit, and it was feared that there were twenty lives lost. But it appears that several of the men were absent from the pit on Tuesday, and it has been ascertained that the total loss will not exceed eighteen – a fearfully long list it must be admitted, but happily falling far short of original expectations. The following is a list of the deceased, all the bodies excepting the last named two having been recovered before the inquest adjourned on Thursday; —

1   John Birchenough, 35, married, three children, Acres Nook, Goldenhill.
2   John Stamper, 27, single, Talke.
3   James Hackney, 16, single, Congleton.
4   Benjamin Booth, 21, single, Talke.
5   Thomas Booth, 46, married, four children, Talke.
6   Thomas Breeze, 26, married, three children, Talke.
7   Thomas William Harrison, 14, Talke.
8   David Winkle, 16, Talke.
9   John Shannon, 19, single, Talke.
10 William Jones, 28, single, Talke.
11 Thomas Grocott, 23 married, one child, Talke.
12 Richard Sherwin, 14, Talke.
13 William Lowndes, 20, single.
14 Robert Walker, 16, Barthomley.
15 John Baynham, 30, married, four children, Talke.
16 Henry Grocott, 27, married, no children, Talke.
17 Francis Birch, 17, Coal-pit Hill.
18 Samuel Kenny, 16, Red Street.

The wonder is that the loss of life was not greater but with the exception of those above, and those who were affected by the afterdamp, few sustained injury. The hooker-on and a boy were blown through a pair of air doors and escaped with slight injuries. Some of the lamps have been found in the eight-foot seam. They have been broken by the explosion

171

but have not been tampered with. The body of the fireman who was supposed to have fired the shot, was found alongside that of another man, they having apparently started to run together after the shot was fired. The deceased are described as being steady and industrious work people. Three of them were Good Templars and some of them were members of the North Staffordshire Provident Association, while others have been subscribers to the Coal and Ironworkers' Relief Fund, the latter showing that they were superior to the narrow prejudice which prevents such a large number of the colliers of the district from subscribing for the benefits conferred partly by the benevolent six years ago, partly by the employers of the present day, added to the small subscription which the men need pay themselves.

Such a sad occurrence naturally created great consternation in the village, and, as the news spread in an exaggerated form throughout the district, large crowds including the excited friends of those employed in the pit, surrounded the mouth of the pit, many of them audibly manifesting their sorrow.

As evening advanced the crowd got thinner till there were few left excepting the policemen on duty; but on Wednesday hundreds of persons from distant places visited the pit bank, and the Swan Inn, where most of the bodies were laid out.

Amongst the visitors on Wednesday were the Mayor of Hanley, (E. F. Bodley Esq.) and Mr. J. G. Walker, manager of the District Bank at Hanley, who made a timely offer of a sum of money from a fund raised over what was required for the relief of the friends of those who were killed by the explosion at the same pit in 1866, and from which £50 was recently sent to the Pelsall relief committee. A more fitting application could not be made of the surplus of the funds raised in Hanley six years ago.

The Rev. W. M. McHutchin, vicar of Talke, who, with other Nonconformist ministers and other gentlemen exerted themselves to console the bereaved and excited people on Tuesday, has received the following letter from the Bishop of Lichfield;

Lollard's Towers, Lambeth, London, S.E.
19th February 1873

" *My dear Mr. McHutchin, – I am shocked to see in the Times of this morning the report of another dreadful colliery accident. My mind is still full of the thoughts of Pelsall. Pray take some opportunity of assuring the widows and orphans of my sympathy with them in their bereavement, and apply the enclosed cheque (for £5) for their benefit in any way that you think best.*

Yours, very faithfully, G.A. Lichfield."

The following letter has been received by the vicar from Sir Smith Child, Bart. M.P.

Carlton Club, Pall Mall, London. 19th Feb.

"My Dear Sir, – I am very sorry to see by the paper that there has been another terrible accident at Talke. I shall be glad to hear particulars. I asked Mr. Bruce in the House of Commons about it, but he knows nothing yet. Did you not tell me some time back that some of the leaders of the Colliers' Union had been publicly speaking against the Miners' Relief Society and advised the men not to join? I should think there might be something spared from the former

Talke Fund, and there is the remains of the Hartley Fund, amounting to several hundreds, which is available. Mr. R. Heath and Mr. Goddard are the newly appointed trustees of this fund; application should be made to them at once I think. I asked them for the surplus for the Relief Association but Mr. Heath seemed to think that the fund should be applied for similar accidents. Your recent case is, therefore, in point. I sent Mr. Heath's letter to Sir L. T. Stamer. He is at 81, King's Road, Brighton, I think. – Yours truly, Smith Child."

The inquest on the bodies of the fifteen men and boys recovered was opened at the Swan Inn, Talke, on Thursday morning before Mr. J. Booth, Coroner. The inquest was attended by Mr. Hugh Birley, M.P., and Mr. Roseby, two of the directors of the company; Mr. Shute, the consulting engineer; Mr. Hunter, the manager of the works; and superintendent Longdon. Mr. Welch, solicitor, watched the proceedings on the part of the friends of some of the deceased and the Amalgamated Association of Miners. Mr. Sherratt, solicitor, attended on behalf of the proprietors of the colliery.

The Coroner, addressing the jury, said that they were called together to inquire into the deaths of the persons who were killed by the explosion in the colliery of the North Staffordshire Coal and Iron Company on the 15th inst. At present he had but little information with regard to the explosion, except that fifteen men were known to be dead and three others were supposed to be dead from the effects of it. This was the same colliery in which an explosion took place in December 1866, when 91 men and boys were killed. He did not propose to go into the case that day. He should take evidence of the explosion and of the identification of the bodies, and then adjourn for some time in order to procure evidence as to the state of the mine, and to enable the jury to arrive at a reasonable conclusion as to the cause of the accident. Mr. Wynne, Government Inspector of Mines was in London attending a meeting. He had telegraphed to Mr. Wynne, but had not received an answer and did not know how long it would take Mr. Wynne to go over the mine and form an opinon of the cause of the accident.

Mr. Birley said that a telegram had been received from Mr. Wynne saying that he would be with them "in the morning", but it was uncertain whether Thursday or Friday was meant.

The first witness called was Henry Blood, collier, living at Tunstall, who said he knew the deceased John Birchenough, who was a roadmaster. He was 36 years old and worked at the Talke colliery. His dead body was in the room upstairs.

John Graham, of Talke, deputy fireman, said he worked in the pit in question on Tuesday last. He began work at eight o' clock that morning. He examined all the places in the new eight foot seam, and they were all right and free from gas. He went into the pit after the explosion. He and others found Breeze and Baynham. Both were dead. Breeze's lamp was about twenty yards from him. The damp was so bad that they moved back. They also found Shannon. Witness knew John Stamper, whose body was lying at this house. Stamper lodged at witness's house.

The foreman; "I should like to know what is meant by deputy fireman."

Witness said that he looked after the bratticing, saw to the firing and also saw that the turnsmen kept to their work.

The Coroner; – "The pit was worked by single shift."

By Mr. Welch; – Witness found Breeze twenty yards from his lamp. The lamp was further into the working than the body. –

By the Coroner; – "The explosion happened in the new eight foot seam."

By Mr. Welch; – "Mr. Halliday had the supervision of both the 7 foot and the 8 foot seams."

Sarah Franklin, wife of Frederick Franklin, collier, New road, said that James Hackney had been lodging at her house. Hackney worked at No. 1 pit of the colliery in question. His dead body was with the others upstairs.

John Berrisford, miner, Butt Lane, said Benjamin Booth had been lodging at his mother's house. He was 21 years old. He worked at No.1 pit. His dead body was lying upstairs.

The Rev. George Jones, Primitive Methodist minister, Talke, said he knew Thomas Breeze, who was 25 years old. Breeze worked at the No. 1 pit. He identified Breeze as one of the deceased.

Alice Podmore, New Road, said she knew Thomas Wm. Harris, who was 14 years old, and was amongst the deceased.

James Hilditch, blacksmith, said he knew David Winkle, who was 15 years old. He worked at the No.1 pit. He was killed by the explosion on Tuesday.

Wm. Jackson, check weighman, spoke as to the death of Shannon, who was 19 years old. He was employed by the workmen and kept their check against the employers. The witness also identified Thomas Booth, aged 31.

Sarah Roberts, wife of a collier, living at Alsager's Bank, gave evidence of the death of Wm. Jones aged 28 years.

Wm. Rogers, collier, the Hollins, identified the body of Thomas Grocott, who was 20 years old.

Thomas Sherwin, father of Richard Sherwin, said his son worked at No.1 pit, and was amongst those who were killed there on Tuesday last.

Mrs. Lowndes identified the body of her stepson Wm. Lowndes, aged 20 years. The witness was aided in her identification of the body by a tobacco-box found in deceased's pocket

Mary Cotton stated that Robert Walker was her son. He was

amongst those who were killed by the explosion.

Richard Hazlehurst said he worked down the ten-foot seam of the colliery in question. He knew John Baynham, who worked in the seam where the explosion occurred. He was killed.

Edwin Durber, morning fireman in the seven and eight-foot seams, said he took the seven-foot first and the eight-foot second for the purpose of examination. Then returned to the bottom to tell Halliday, the overman. On Tuesday he went down about half past two o'clock. He examined the working places and found them all right. There was no trace of gas in either seam. There was no gas in the drift gobs. It was about five o' clock – perhaps a little later – when he got back to the pit bottom. Witness was 25 years old and had been fireman since the first week in January. When he got to the pit bottom he waited for Halliday. Witness made an entry in the book before he saw Halliday, who went down the pit about half past five o' clock. To the best of his recollection what he wrote in the book was "I have examined all the places in the seven and eight-foot seams, and found them all right." When

Halliday came down witness said to him, "They're all right," and he replied, "That's right." Witness left the pit at half past ten o'clock. John Graham took witness off the seven-foot seam at eight o'clock, and Thomas Breeze took him off the other seam at half past five. They were firing shots before witness left. The shots were in cartridges and the fuse was fired through the gauze of the lamps, the tops not being taken off. They were all gauze lamps. Witness only fired three or four shots. Breeze's duty was to go round the workings to see if there was any gas. He told Breeze all was right in the eight-foot seam. Witness had seen gas in the eight-foot seam twice since he had been fireman. When he saw gas he registered it if he was on duty. If he made an incorrect register the next man would have detected it. He had once found a little gas and had entered the fact in a book at the bottom of the pit, but not in the book on the pit bank. That was the only matter about which any complaint had been made against him.

By Mr. Welch; – "There was a thirling from the back drift to the heading or level above, where a man was working the day before.

When he saw it the morning of the explosion there was a little air going up, just to keep the place clear. The place was clear of gas."

By the Coroner; – "He knew Birchenough. He did not know that Birchenough had a right to have a lamp key."

The inquest was then adjourned, but the jury re-assembled at a quarter to four in the afternoon, the body of Henry Grocott having been brought up a few minutes previously. John Grocott identified the body of the deceased who was a distant relative. The body was found at the top of the workings where it had been buried in rafters the drift having fallen on the deceased.

The inquest was further adjourned till today.

On Thursday night the body of Birch was brought from the pit, Kenny's body being the only one undiscovered.

Yesterday Mr. T. Wynne visited the mine, but did not complete his examination.

The bodies of Winkle, Jones, Breeze and Henry Grocott were interred at Talke, the officiating minister being W.M. McHutchin, vicar.

THE COLLIERY EXPLOSION AT TALKE.

Last week we gave particulars of the catastrophe by which 18 lives were lost at the colliery at Talke, belonging to the North Staffordshire Coal and Iron Company. Our report concluded with the statement that, of the 18 persons known to be dead, only one of the bodies — that of Samuel Kenyon,* aged 15 — remained undiscovered, and that five of the bodies which had been found were, on Friday, interred in Talke Churchyard.

Late on Friday night Kenyon's body was found beneath a large heap of debris near the place where he had worked. It was not much crushed and, excepting for the face, but little burnt. On Saturday the inquest was re-opened and evidence was given as to the identity of the bodies of Birch and Kenyon, so that the Coroner might make an order for their burial. The inquiry was then again adjourned. A wish was expressed by some of the jurors that four of their number, who were practical colliers should, in the interval, make an examination of the eight foot seam, where the accident took place, with a view to assisting the jury in arriving at a conclusion as to the cause of the explosion. The Coroner approved the suggestion, and Mr. Hunter, the manager of the colliery, at once offered to place every facility in the way of carrying it out. The ventilation of the pit is fully restored so that, with the exception of the eight foot seam (which will remain until after the inquest in nearly the same condition it was in immediately after the explosion) the mine may be worked, indeed the men have, during the past week, re-commenced operations in other parts of the pit. We have already mentioned that four of the bodies were interred in Talke Churchyard on Friday afternoon. On Saturday afternoon six more, and on Sunday afternoon five others, were buried in Talke Churchyard. The obsequies attracted a considerable number of persons, and large numbers of friends and relatives were in the funeral processions. The coffins were met at the churchyard gate

---

* Kenyon is spelt variously as Kenny, Kenyon and Kennion. His father was killed in the 1866 explosion and is listed as Kennion.

by the vicar, the Rev. W. M. McHutchin and the curate the Rev. J. R. Barnes, who performed the funeral rites in the church and at the graves. The local Good Templars joined in the procession of young Sherwin's friends, he having belonged to that order, and, out of respect to Wm. Lowndes, the Chesterton Brass Band to which he had belonged, followed

his remains and played the "Dead March". Birchenough, Hackney and Walker were buried in other places. The colliery company have defrayed the expenses of all the funerals, and intend to materially assist the bereaved. The fathers of Harrison and Kenyon were amongst the 91 persons killed by the explosion in the same pit in 1866.

CHAPTER FOURTEEN

STAFFORDSHIRE DAILY SENTINEL 3RD MAY 1875

THE COLLIERY EXPLOSION
AT
TALK-O'-TH'-HILL

FORTY-THREE LIVES LOST.
In our issue of Saturday we published a tolerably full account of the fearful explosion at Bunker's Hill Colliery belonging to Messrs Rigby & Co. which occurred on Friday afternoon *(Sic.30th April)* at one o'clock. It is not infrequently the case in disasters of this kind that the circumstances get over-stated, yet quite unintentionally. In the excitement and effort which inevitably succeed a colliery explosion of anything like the character of that at Bunker's Hill there is often difficulty found in obtaining information and those people who read the newspaper reports have but little idea of the great amount of work involved in obtaining particulars, of the patient waiting, the judicious questioning and the anxious enquiring necessary before an account can be shaped to present to the public. In some cases those connected with the colliery are so reticent that it is with the utmost difficulty items of information can be obtained. In reference to the explosion at Bunker's Hill Colliery no such difficulty was experienced. It was quite the contrary and we would at once acknowledge the readiness manifested by Mr. Rigby and those connected with the colliery to supply all needful information. The police officials, it may also be mentioned, were - as indeed they invariably are in this district - most courteous and helpful to the members of the press, so that all channels were open to get the best information obtainable.

RECOVERY OF THE BODIES
We may take up our narrative of this disaster at the point we finished in our Saturday's version. Unfortunately this disaster has exceeded in magnitude what we then represented. We stated that as far as could be ascertained the list of dead would amount to about thirty-five. The exploring parties, as they ascended, varied in their accounts as to the state of things, and naturally so, for the dead were found in almost all parts of the workings, some in the roadways, some in the dips and some in the "cruts" (crossings from the levels).

The general impression was that from thirty to forty dead bodies were in the Banbury (the eight foot coal seam) where the explosion had occurred. Unfortunately over forty men and boys have perished. The assumption that we had expressed that *all* in the workings had been killed turns out to be correct. Not a soul has escaped to tell the story of how the explosion occurred. Up to about nine o' clock on Friday night some dozen bodies had been recovered. The ventilation of the pit had been fully restored but there was difficulty experienced in pushing along the workings. There was however earnest, undaunted and untiring effort on the part of the explorers, and soon the melancholy business of picking up corpses and conveying them to the bottom of the shaft was carried out with dispatch. The sad nature of the work during the night may be imagined, we confess inability to describe it. From ten o'clock until midnight bodies were sent up as quickly as possible and were conveyed away either to the homes of the deceased or to the Swan Inn at Talke. Until a late hour the pit banks were thronged with spectators and some persons even remained until late on Saturday morning. We understand that the bodies were found in groups of three in about four cases and in one instance four bodies were together. Some appeared to have been hurrying away trying to escape apprehended danger, some to have been sitting down and many had their hands before their eyes as though endeavouring to ward off approaching ill. In that attitude - and with the arms and hands stiffened in death - many of the deceased were found. A number of lamps were discovered but there was no indication of any clue of the cause of the explosion. By five o' clock on Saturday morning what was considered the last of the dead - making forty one bodies - was brought out. During the morning some difficulty was felt in identifying several of the bodies, in consequence of their mutilated state, and there was some apprehension that one or two bodies had been sent to the wrong place. There was special difficulty as to the body of Joseph Ashmore, whose son had been found. That difficulty was not cleared up until afternoon. There was a re-searching of the workings instituted then and the result was the finding of the body of Ashmore at the far end of the workings.

The following is a complete, and we believe, accurate

LIST OF THE DEAD

1   William Maxfield (22),Hall Green, widow, one child.
2   Thomas Lawton (24), Kent's Green, widow, three children.
3   William Hancock (33), Talke Pitts, widow, five children.
4   Enoch Hancock (31), Talke, widow, two children.
5   James Stevenson (15), Talke Pitts.
6   John Buckley (24),Lawton,(Cheshire), widow, two children
7   Caleb Baddaley (24), Talke, single.
8   Daniel Charlesworth (13), Coal Pitt Hill.
9   Thomas Peats (17), New Road, single.
10 David Boston (23), Alsager, widow, one child.
11 John Rogers (16), Alsager.
12 Thomas Thompson (17), Congleton , single.
13 Isaiah Cooper (22), New Road, widow, two children
14 Thomas Beech (23), Lawton Meir, widow, two children.
15 Daniel Fox (35), Lawton Meir, widow, two children.
16 Jesse Nield (21), Butt Lane, widow, one child.
17 Eli Burton (19), Congleton, single.
18 James Boyd (13), Talke.
19 Thomas Holland (33), Talke, widow, two children.
20 John Hancock (18), Talke, single.
21 George Breeze (22), Coal Pit Hill, single.
22 Samuel George Morris (21), New Road, widow, no family.
23 George Holland (44), Meir Lane, widow, ten children.
24 Joseph Chadwick (23), Butt Lane, widow, one child.
25 William Henry Boughey (14) Coal Pit Hill.
26 Henry Dean (42), New Road, widow, five children
27 Thomas Dean (14), New Road.
28 Joseph Holland (26), The Hollins, widow, one child.
29 Levi Ashmore (14), Alsager.
30 Walter Moore (40), Butt Lane, widow, one child.
31 Herbert Moore (13), son of Walter Moore.
32 Richard Dale (13), New Road.
33 James Edward Higgins (20), New Road, single.
34 Richard Jackson (59), Talke, widower, seven children.
35 John Lucas (24), Butt Lane, widow, one child.

36 James Yearsley (27), Butt Lane, widow, two children.
37 Joseph Carter (23,) single, New Road.
38 William Henry Proudlove (15), New Road.
39 John Marshall (17), New Road, single.
40 James Stubbs (18), New Road, single.
41 Thomas Mason (25), Alsager, widow, one child.
42 Joseph Ashmore (45), Alsager, widow, four children
43 Nehemiah Sumner (24), widow, no family.

At one stroke death has thus made twenty- two women widows and fifty-six children fatherless. In a few cases father and son died together. Two of the Hollands were brothers and had only just begun work at the pit. The boy Charlesworth it was said was not quite dead when discovered, but he died as soon as the pit bank was reached. Most of the bodies were found at the extreme end of the workings.

THE CHAMBER OF THE DEAD

In a large room at the Swan Inn there lay on Saturday morning twenty-one dead bodies. They had been washed and placed upon boards in rows, and decently covered with sheets – a sad and pitiful sight certainly. P.S. Torr had for a long time special charge of the room, and free access was accorded to anyone who liked to see the bodies with a view to identification. That was difficult in a few cases for the disfiguration was awful. In the case of Walter Moore, a pit fireman, – who, by the way, is spoken of as having been a most trustworthy man, it was only by his curly hair that he could be identified for his face was literally unrecognisable. In another case it was only by the man's garter that identification could be made. The coroner evinced particular anxiety to secure as satisfactory identification as was possible, and, as far as we could see, that was assuredly done. Some of the visitors to the room were colliers inured to danger, and accustomed to gaze upon death as the fate some of the colliers suffered.

They did not seem at all affected. Others evidenced that to gaze upon death had been a trying matter. Relatives with tearful eyes came down the stairs and their grief evinced sympathy. The Inn was thronged with people during the whole day, and not a few seemed oblivious of the awful surroundings. Possibly, however, the unfortunate frequency of disasters of this kind may have blunted the sensibilities of some. A number of people had come from the Potteries to see and hear all they could and they were not debarred from gratifying any morbid feeling of curiosity they might have to see the bodies of the dead colliers.

OPENING OF THE INQUEST.

On Saturday, Mr. J. Booth, North Staffordshire coroner, reached the pit shortly before eleven o' clock in company with Superintendent Baker and he at once directed that a jury should be summoned as soon as possible at the Swan Inn. The coroner intimated that it was the purpose to simply take evidence as to the identity of the deceased, and then to adjourn the inquiry. The sad business of identification was then proceeded with in the lower room of the Swan. Amongst those present were Mr. Wynne, Government Inspector of Mines, Mr. Offrey, Assistant Inspector, (who had been down the pit with Mr. John Rigby and Mr. Sumner, manager, making an examination of the workings all morning), Rev.

Sir L.T. Stanmer Bart. (who is President of the North Staffordshire Coal and Ironworks Permanent Relief Society) Rev. W.M. MacHutchin, Mr. Rigby, Mr. C.J. Homer, Mr. John Rigby, Dr. Hayes, Chief Superintendent Longden, Superintendent Baker etc. The work of identification lasted well into the afternoon. The only witness who could say a word about the pit was William Stevenson, who was called to identify the body of his son James. He was at work in the eight foot seam at the time of the explosion – ten minutes to one o'clock – but not in the part where it occurred. He heard a noise which he thought at the time being so far distant from it, was a fall of roof. He did not think an explosion had occurred. It did not affect his light. He had worked at the colliery about twenty years. During that period the ventilation of the mine had always been very good. The coroner; Did you see any gas at all on your side on the day of the explosion? Witness; I have not seen a bit of gas the last five years. There was difficulty found in identifying one of the bodies in the room. There was nothing about the clothing to connect them with Joseph Ashmore. It was therefore apparent that another body must be in the pit. Even while the jury were sitting searching in the pit was again instituted, and the body of Ashmore was found. The remains were brought to the Swan, and the dead list was then swelled to forty-two. The inquest was adjourned to the 12th. Inst.

Staffordshire Daily Sentinel, 13ᵗʰ May 1875

LATER REPORT

INCIDENTS.

How the work of death was done and the causes will probably remain a mystery though a theory probably not far from the truth is likely to be presented. It is not long since the practice of blasting has taken the place of coal getting by the 'wedging' system. The strong assumption is that the explosion was caused by the firing of a shot. Some of the colliers had a strong opinion that the coal dust was fired. Walter Moore, whose record of the pit being free from gas and the ventilation good when he made his examination in the morning was among the killed. The first to descend to begin the work of exploration was Mr. Sumner, the manager, and Mr. Charles Lawton, underground manager at the North Staffordshire Coal and Iron Company's Colliery at Talke. Mr. W. Branson subsequently rendered good service in the work of exploration. Messrs. Lawton and Branson we understand were among the foremost to risk their lives in rescuing the bodies of their fellow workmen at the disastrous explosion which occurred at Talke in 1866, continuing in their noble work for 36 hours in succession. Again in the 1873 explosion they were among the explorers and narrowly escaped with their lives. Scores of volunteers to form exploring parties were ready at hand willing and anxious to assist in the work. There was special sadness about the incidents of the first descent. Nehemiah Sumner, son of the manager was the first person met with. He at the time of the explosion was blown with great violence against some timbers at the bottom of the shaft, and besides being seriously burnt was so badly injured that his life was considered in the greatest danger. He was married but a fortnight since, and was a very respectable steady man. One of the lads who was killed only went down the pit two hours before the accident, taking the place of another lad who had gone home too unwell to work. Enoch Hancock commenced work in the pit the day before, his brother, William Hancock, entering upon an engagement on Wednesday. Both they and their uncles, George and Thomas Holland were among the killed. Several of the victims were men who had previously worked at the Rodney Bush Colliery, on the other side of the hill, which had fallen in and been abandoned only the previous Saturday. Some of the men in the other working, on hearing the explosion rushed towards the shaft and received injuries by stumbling against projections in their way but none are seriously hurt. In several cases fathers and sons perished together. Daniel Charlesworth's boy was brought to the bank alive but died almost immediately. He had perished from the after-damp and had not been burnt. In most cases death appeared to have been instantaneous. These persons were found lying on their faces as they had been struck down by either fire or after-damp, and had

immediately succumbed. Some had made attempts to escape, but in the darkness had lost their way, and were unable to get beyond the reach of the deadly enemy. One lad, who, though not in the lower part of the dip, happened to be within reach of the after-damp, is said to have been saved by cramming his cap into his mouth.

On Saturday morning a number of people found their way to the colliery, but there was nothing about the pit beyond its ordinary aspect. During the morning the four dead horses were got out. Rain fell during the greater part of the day, and although very welcome for the dry ground, tended to increase the depressing influence of the locality. It was particularly saddening to observe while passing through Butt Lane, New Road and Talke the drawn blinds at so many houses, indicative of the great tragedy that had occurred. The coffins for the dead were supplied by Mr. Rigby.

There was great excitement at Talke yesterday and the colliery was visited by some thousands of people, but no interments took place in the churchyard there.

Fifteen of the deceased were connected with the North Staffordshire Coal and

Ironworkers' Permanent Relief Society.

DEATH OF NEHEMIAH SUMNER

We have received intelligence of the death this morning of Nehemiah Sumner, son of the manager. He was twenty-four years old.

Charles Lawton in Derbyshire

CHAPTER FIFTEEN

ENDPIECE

TO DERBYSHIRE

In 1883, at the age of 44, Charles Lawton moved to Ripley in Derbyshire to take the position of Manager at Ford's Marehay Main Colliery. He had worked underground at Talke-o'-th'-Hill colliery in Staffordshire for 36 years during which time he had experienced dreadful conditions and witnessed catastrophic disasters. Leading the rescuing bands on more than one occasion he earned the respect and praise of Government Mine Inspectors, employers and work mates for his bravery and persistence in searching, often for many hours among the debris, for survivors. The unique geology of the coal seams in Staffordshire meant that extracting coal was always difficult, requiring a special technique, as described in Chapter 2. The risks were great and the threat of underground fire and explosion was faced daily by the courageous men who toiled in unimaginable conditions to wrench the valuable fossil from the bowels of the earth. It was said, at the time, that anyone who could work in a Staffordshire pit could work anywhere. Lawton had several times reached the end of his tether but always the promise of promotion weakened his resolve and he remained loyal to his employers, the owners of Talke-o'-th'-Hill.

Eventually he was lured away to Derbyshire and took up residence at Chapel Street, Ripley with his wife Elizabeth and daughter Hannah who was then eighteen. At this time Hannah remained his favourite. She was the baby of the family, born when the family was thriving, eight years after her next oldest sibling, Lilla and fifteen years after the first born, Matilda. Her father's pet name for her was Nancy. She married some years later a man of whom her father did not approve. After that there was little contact between them, although, of his three daughters, she was the only one to benefit from his will. Hannah was my granny but my mother, her daughter Christina never spoke of her grandfather. It would appear that he never visited their humble home with its outside toilet, black-leaded cooking range and a cast iron pump, cold water only, over the stone sink in the kitchen. In my granny's lifetime the house was never altered. I remember it so well. My strongest childhood memory is of Granny Irving sitting, cat Twink on her knee, in her rocking chair beside

189

The Harbour – c.1920.

The Harbour, 1993, now derelict. Swan Bank, Talke.

191

the fire. A copy of Charles Lawton's will was among the papers passed
to me on the death of my aunt. Part is reproduced below.

*'I will that the whole (of my estate) be sold or
so arranged by them (the executors) as to be
divisible into equal parts for the use and enjoyment
of the following named persons absolutely. Mr.
Frank Lawton (my son) of Ripley, Derbyshire, Mr.
Luther Lawton (my son) of Ripley Derbyshire, Mrs.
Hannah Irving (my daughter) the wife of Robert
Irving of Over Lane near Belper and that they take
share and share alike. Note. To my other two
daughters I leave no interest or any part in this my
will they having for some years past disowned me.'*

Charles Lawton took up his position as Manager, at Ford's Marehay
Main Colliery, on January 29 1883. His move may have been
precipitated by the appointment of Mr. Nicholls as Under-Manager.
Lawton writes in "A Reminiscence of a Colliers Life" at the time of the
1866 explosion,

*'my overman was the brother-in-law of the
Manager. He was totally unfit for the office.'*

This opinion was reinforced in government inspector Wynne's report
of the explosion to the Home Office. Lawton was not a man to endure
such a relationship. It is interesting to note that Lawton's son-in-law
Albert Mayon Henshaw later took over as Manager of Talke-o'-th'-Hill
becoming Managing Director in 1898. He had married Matilda, or Tilly
as she was known in the family, the daughter who was Charles' first
child when he was just 19 years of age. Tilly and Albert moved into The
Harbour, Kidsgrove, now sadly derelict and overlooking a supermarket.
In those days, as befitted the Manager's house, it was an imposing
residence with servants' accommodation and an impressive stable block
to the rear of a spacious garden. It overlooked, from a distance, the
pithead. Albert himself was a prestigious character in the mining world
and was featured in the *'Colliery Guardian'* of September 19, 1924 as *"A*

MEN OF NOTE in the BRITISH COAL INDUSTRY.

(With Supplement Plate.)

No. 38.—Mr. A. M. HENSHAW.

Eldest son of late John Henshaw, of the Kingswood and Parkfield Collieries, Bristol, Mr. Henshaw was educated at Merchant Venturers' Technical College, Bristol, and was articled as pupil at Kingswood Collieries, Bristol, and Collins Green and Bold Collieries, Lancashire. His first position of responsibility was that of manager of Talk o'-th'-Hill Collieries, Staffordshire, of which he has been managing director since 1898. Mr. Henshaw at an early date became associated with Dr. Haldane in his work on Spontaneous Combustion and the effects of Carbon Monoxide, and with Sir W. N. Atkinson, in the investigation of explosions, notably at Courrières, in the Pas-de-Calais. With the latter he was joint author of papers on that calamity and the investigation of colliery explosions. He was awarded a gold medal for services at the disastrous fire at Hamstead Colliery in 1908, and holds the silver medal of the North Staffordshire Mines Rescue Association. Mr. Henshaw has had a large experience of and is a recognised authority on explosions, spontaneous combustion, coal dust, and kindred subjects, contributing to literature, and giving evidence before Royal Commission and Departmental Committees. As a practical mining engineer, he is equally well known in all our coal fields. He was one of the first to adopt rescue apparatus, using the original Meyer oxygen apparatus for exploration work at the Talk o'-th'-Hill explosion in 1901, and was one of the pioneers of "Safety First" in mines, instituting the movement at Talk o'-th'-Hill in 1913, with signal success. Mr. Henshaw has been engaged in the recovery of by-products of coal since 1889. His appointments include the following: director, Staffordshire Chemical Co., Ltd.; director, New Acid Co., Ltd., Staffordshire; member of the Safety in Mines Research Board; central examiner appointed by the Board for Mining Examinations; external examiner in mining, University of Leeds; past president, North Staffs. Institute of Mining and Mechanical Engineers; past president North Staffs. Colliery Owners' Association; past president, North Staffs. Association of Colliery Managers; member, Institution of Civil Engineers; Fellow, Geological Society of London; J.P., County of Staffordshire.

Albert Mayon Henshaw,
husband of Matilda (Tilly) Lawton

'Endpiece'

Man of Note in the British Coal Mining Industry". In collaboration with
Dr. Haldane, he wrote papers on the investigation of colliery explosions.
He was awarded a Gold Medal for services rendered at the disastrous fire
at Hamstead colliery in 1908. He holds the silver medal of the North
Staffordshire Mines Rescue Association. Recognised as an authority on
explosions, spontaneous combustion and coal dust he was one of the first
to adopt the Meyer oxygen breathing apparatus for exploration work at
Talke-o'-th'-Hill in 1901. He was one of the pioneers of 'Safety First' in
mines, instigating the movement with great success at Talke in 1913. All
of these qualifications should have endeared him to Charles Lawton
who, as a direct result of his first hand experiences, would have shared
his interest and concern. However there appears to have been a serious
difference of opinion and Tilly was cut out of her father's will. Neither of
the Henshaws, nor their two children attended Charles' funeral nor did
they send floral tributes.

   Charles Lawton was not universally popular at Ford's and seems to
have crossed swords with some of the workforce very shortly after he
took control. I have used as my source *"The Journal of a Derbyshire
Pitman 1835 - 1906"* by Terry Judge. When I was first deliberating about
what to do with Lawton's original hand written document I was directed
to Terry, a local mining historian and he was extremely helpful. He
accompanied me on a visit to Kidsgrove and Butt Lane where Lawton
was born and he gave me a copy of his book to use for reference. His
book takes the form of a diary written by Derbyshire coal-miner Joseph
Wright who worked at Ford's Marehay Main pit at the time that Lawton
was manager. Joseph and his brother George were soon in trouble
incurring the manager's wrath by falsely claiming coal allowances that
were not due to them and defrauding the company. Colliers were entitled
to a certain number of free loads of house coals per year for which they
only paid 'carting' It was a serious offence to embezzle coal and the
manager was within his rights to enforce instant dismissal. On June 9
they were both given fourteen days' notice but they left the next day.
This infuriated Lawton. Never one to forgive and forget, when Joseph
went to talk to him many months later about his dismissal he was told *'it
all arises from the coal ticket affair'* and the grievance about
giving up the *'ganging contract'*. In July 1884 Joseph Wright applied

194

for the *'getting out contract'* at the mine. Lawton refused to pay him the going rate for the job. Instead Mr. Bradley was employed. Within a few days Joseph was recalled because Bradley, the *'getter out'*, had injured his leg and been *'taken home on a cart'*. As the elected representative of the workforce, a sort of latter day shop steward, Joseph Wright was always a thorn in the flesh of Manager Lawton. He was rebellious and spoke up for the men against the harsh conditions imposed by the manager and the owners. Joseph Wright did not say much that was good about Charles Lawton.

Records show that Charles Lawton was manager at Ford's Marehay Main pit for almost 25 years, retiring at the ripe old age of 69. This in itself is remarkable for those times when pit disasters were commonplace and little was known of the health risks inherent in the dreadful underground conditions. Remember that Charles left school aged 8 years, working as pit boy for 2 years. He went underground at the tender age of 10 years to spend the next 34 years in one of the most dangerous and fiery pits in the country, many times risking his own life attempting to rescue others. During this time he educated himself and worked tirelessly to improve the lot of the coal-miners. He especially concentrated his efforts on ensuring managers and owners obeyed the law, forbidding boys under 12 years of age to work underground. He spoke vehemently in support of the move to get women and girls brought out of the pits altogether although it still bothered him that they were employed in undignified heavy pit head tasks and were subjected to all forms of abuse from 'coarse and ignorant men'. He also writes,

'The collier's wife and the collier's daughter shall no longer go into the mines to be degraded and abused by their lords and masters worse than ordinary beasts of burden.'

His great concern and respect for women may well have had its foundation in his early life when his mother struggled on her own to bring him up and care for him. He certainly adored and cherished her, writing very lovingly, of his *'dear mother'* moved by her tears as she *'cried while she dressed my raw shoulders with salt and water*

195

'Endpiece'

to make them hard.' This to assuage the effects of the cruel 'bite' that he describes so graphically in his story.

Charles Lawton's reputation as an expert on pit safety and rescue procedures led to his election to the founding membership of the Institute of Mining and Mechanical Engineers in 1872. It is possible that his *'A Reminiscence of a Collier's Life'* is the text of an address to the membership of this organisation it was certainly intended as a declamation from some public platform. He was much in demand as a public speaker and lecturer on his highly specialised topic.

Charles Lawton recognised more than most the value of education. He had done it the hard way with little time, encouragement or resources. His facility with the English language, although his text is littered with inaccuracies of spelling, is a fitting testament to his dedication and application to his studies. His interest in the welfare of the rising generation led him to volunteer his services as Secretary of the local Science and Art Classes and of the County Council Classes, a position he held for six years.

Apart from his work to improve conditions in his workplace Charles devoted a considerable amount of his time to community work. On 18 April 1903 he was elected, by a large majority vote, to the first Urban District Council. The same year he became a Guardian of Babington Union and served conscientiously, missing very few meetings until 1907. He served on the School Board, was a voluntary School Manager and served for a while on the Burial Board in the town of Ripley.

In 1906 his beloved wife Elizabeth died aged 72.She was five years his senior and he was to spend the next 15 years without her. In his *'A Reminiscence of a Collier's Life'* he writes,

'Do you see I had then married a wife to help me — to help me with a kind word when I could not get one elsewhere; to help me in every honourable resolve and righteous purpose; to help me by making my few daily wants her constant study; to help me with a smile when the days were dark. She was one of the daughters who could prophecy,

196

saying, "There's a good time a coming lad. Wait a little longer".'

He missed her and was lonely without her. He employed a housekeeper and in 1907 moved to a house in Matlock where he hoped to enjoy full retirement. This does not seem to have worked out too well. He was soon to return, on his own, to take up residence with his son Luther at 30 Ivy Grove, Ripley where he remained until his death in 1921 at the grand old age of 82. He left a special bequest to Eliza, Luther's wife, in gratitude,

'having for many years been my faithful friend under very trying conditions and continued her kindness and found for me many comforts even into my old age'.

Active about the town until a few weeks before his death, Charles was buried in Ripley cemetery on Saturday 9 July 1921. He shares a plot with Elizabeth.

This is the story of a remarkable man who rose through all sorts of adversity and difficulty, educating himself on the way, to a position of authority and respect in his field of endeavour, the infamous coal-mines of the mid 19th century. Not any old coal-mine at that but one in the Staffordshire coal field where fiery pits were the norm and working conditions among the most hazardous. He was moved to write about his experiences. I have tried to fill in the gaps and convey something of the essence of my great grandfather, Charles Lawton. His words, even at a distance of more than a hundred years, have the power to stir the emotions. They direct our thoughts to the suffering and hardships that were the daily round for the men who hewed the coal that supported the national economy and brought comfort and cheer to every home in the land from the humblest hearth to the mansions of the landed gentry.

There are, however, two sides to every coin. As I researched deeper into the contemporary newspaper reports of the explosions and the subsequent inquests and later studied closely the Mining Inspector's Report to The Home Office, I realised that almost certainly great grandpa Lawton had been, to say the least, rather selective in his account of his exploits. I found nothing that would detract from his bravery and courage

DEATH OF FORMER RIPLEY COLLIERY MANAGER.

MR. CHARLES LAWTON, OF IVY GROVE.

Yet another of Ripley's well-respected and oldest residents has passed over to the Great Beyond this week in Mr. Charles Lawton, who early yesterday (Thursday) morning breathed his last at the residence of his son, Mr. Luther Lawton, of Ivy Grove.

Deceased, who was 82 years of age, had been medically attended at intervals for the past few years, but was wonderfully active and energetic, and right up to a little over a week before his death was about the town and interesting himself in securing for the local Gas Co., of which he was a director for fifteen years, five of which as chairman, a supply of coal sufficient to tide them over the coal dispute.

As a colliery manager, first in Staffordshire, the county of his birth, and later at Messrs. Fords' Marehay Main Pits, where he was for about 25 years, retiring a little over thirteen years ago, Mr. Lawton was highly esteemed and in his day was an authority on mining matters. As a lecturer he was most interesting and instructive, and at one time was in great request at the then Mutual Improvement Societies which abounded in the district.

Perhaps no man knew and appreciated more the value of education, and he interested himself so much in the welfare of the rising generation that for six years he undertook the secretaryship of the local Science and Art Classes and of the County Council Classes.

In the year 1903 Mr. Lawton was returned by the electorate to the Urban Council, and in the same year was elected a Guardian. He had also served a span on the School Board, and as a Voluntary School Manager, and for some time was a member of the Burial Board.

In 1907 he went into retirement at Matlock, but later returned to the town in which he had spent the most useful part of his life, and although he had not taken any active part in the management of the town's affairs for a many years he always kept up a lively interest in the fortunes of Ripley.

The interment takes place to-morrow (Saturday) at the General Cemetery at 2 p.m.

Ripley & Heanor News
Funeral Announcement clipping, Friday July 15th 1921

THE LATE MR. CHARLES LAWTON.

FUNERAL AT RIPLEY.

The remains of the late Mr. Charles Lawton, of Ivy Grove, who died on Thursday morning last, and whose death was fully reported in last week's "News," were laid to rest in Ripley Cemetery last Saturday amidst many manifestations of respect.

The bearers were old officials and workmen who were identified with deceased whilst manager at Ford's, viz., Messrs. B. Burton, W. Burton, Geo. Taylor, H. Bonsall, H. Hallam, and Geo. Lancashire.

The mourners were as follows: Messrs. Frank and Luther Lawton (sons), Messrs. Charles Lawton, James Lawt * F. Rhead, and Harry Rhead (grandsons), Mr. Robt. Irving (son-in-law), Mr. D. Rhead (son-in-law), Mr. Abt. Walker, Mr. Thos. Bonstall, Mr. Hy. Stanley, Mr. Saml. Allsop, Mr. Bridgett, Mr. Marshall, Mr. W. Hatfield (Gas Works). The manager and directors of the Gas Co. were represented by Mr. Harding (manager), and Messrs. Ellis-Fermor, G. J. Beighton, and A. E. S. Daykin (directors). There also followed: Messrs. Robt. Aldred (Ford's undermanager), H. Lamb, Jos. Statham, Herbert Statham, Wm. Lilley, Jos. Bowmer, Wm. Aldred, Saml. Beeson.

The Vicar (Rev. E. T. Pegg) conducted the service. Mr. F. S. Allsop supplied the carriages, and Mr. Sam Norman was undertaker.

Floral tributes were as follows: With love and deep sympathy, Frank, Pollie, and family; With sincere sympathy, Luther, Eliza, Florrie, and Abt. (harp); With sincere sympathy, Hannah and Bob; In affectionate remembrance of dear old Grandpa, from his Grandchildren, Bessie and Albert (chaplet); Asleep in Jesus, from his loving Grand-daughter, Lizzie (spray); With sincere sympathy, from Charles Ford, Hastings; A token of remembrance, from C. F. V. Ford, Ripley; With sincere sympathy, from the Directors of the Ripley Gas Co.; With deep sympathy, from Staff and Workmen, Ripley Gas Co.; In loving remembrance, from the Deputies at Ford's Colliery; With deepest sympathy, Mr. and Mrs. Dodd; With deepest sympathy, from Neighbours and Friends of Ivy Grove and bun.

as leader of the rescuing bands, searching for days underground, initially for survivors and later for bodies of workmates lost in the disaster, but some disturbing facts did come to light.

Lawton was deputy undermanager at Talke in 1866. His immediate superior was Mr. Nicholls, a man for whom he had little respect. Both were heavily criticised for the serious lack of discipline underground. We must remember, perhaps in mitigation, that Lawton was only twenty-seven years old at the time and he was put in a position of authority over hardened colliers several years his senior. Discipline underground had been lax for many years and he simply allowed custom and practice to prevail. We read, in the Staffordshire Sentinel report of 2nd February 1867 that unauthorised men were allowed to 'fire shots', many had lamp keys to which they were not entitled and others tampered with their lamps in order to light their pipes and have an illicit smoke. One even claimed to have been given a light from the lamp of Lawton himself. Lawton allowed powder for shots to be carried underground, in fact a witness said that Lawton sold powder to men not qualified to use it. These were flagrant breaches of existing safety rules. Perfect examples of familiarity breeding contempt. The coroner, in his summing up is very severe, pondering on the irresponsible behaviour of Mr. Nicholls, using words such as 'reckless', and 'careless' even considering whether or not a charge of manslaughter would be appropriate. In his final verdict he expresses his regret to see, "the culpable negligence of James Bossons and Charles Lawton in violating the rules made for the protection of life and property in the pit". However he also pays tribute to these two same men for their heroic rescue efforts.

The life of the miner was dire, conditions underground horrendous. Who can criticise him for seeking a little respite and relief. They were a hard and lawless bunch and most pit disasters at this time were a direct result of their cavalier attitude to safety rules that they were supposed to read before they ever ventured underground. The fire of 1866 was identified by the coroner as being caused by, 'a naked light'. It is obvious that much blame lies at the doors of Mr. Nicholls, Undermanager and his deputy, Charles Lawton. In fact the latter narrowly escaped a charge of culpable negligence. The load of guilt that lay on his shoulders may well have been the catalyst for his evangelical campaign for improved safety in the mines. Credit is due to him for overcoming this most serious failure and for using the experience to enlighten others and change attitudes to safety underground for all the miners that followed him.

Today's society is so litigious that every aspect of our lives is encompassed by Health and Safety legislation. Children can no longer play 'conkers' in the school playground unless they wear protective goggles, Bring and Buy sales, church fetes and local village fund-raising events cannot sell home-made cakes which are not packaged to give a full list of ingredients and insurance premiums for any 'activity' event are prohibitive. Safety at Work is every employer's mantra and he is penalised heavily and rightly for neglecting to ensure that his workforce has adequate protection. It is hard for us to appreciate the uncertainty and worry that attended the miners and their families every working day. These close knit communities lived with fear and when tragedy struck hardly anyone was untouched by it. Many families would have lost the breadwinner and many more had sacrificed wage – earning sons. We have read in this account of instances where both fathers and sons succumbed in the same disaster. Families helped and supported each other and relied on the generosity of the church and other benefactors to get them through the hard times. Community spirit then was stronger than anything that could be found today.

I wanted to collect together, in one volume, the Reminiscences of a working miner, Charles Lawton my Great Grandfather, with the objective accounts from contemporary newspapers and Government Inspectors' reports; in an attempt to present a rounded picture of the coal industry of the 19th century. I have found the subject absorbing, shocking and moving. I hope I have been able to transmit some of those emotions to the reader.

Charles Lawton

Gravestone of Elizabeth and Charles Lawton in Ripley Cemetery

The young lambs are bleating in the meadows
The young birds are chirping in their nests
The young fawns are playing with the shadows
The young flowers are blowing toward the west
But the young. young children. Oh My Brothers
They are weeping bitterly
Weeping in the play time of the others
In the country of the free

Go out Children from the mines and from the city
Sing out Children as the little Thrushes do
Pluck your handfulls of the meadow cowslips pretty
Laugh aloud to feel your fingers let them through
But they answer – Are your Cowslips of the meadows
Like our weeds anear the mine
Leave us quiet in the dark of the Coal Shadows
From your pleasures fair and fine

For Oh said the Children · we are weary
For we can not run or leap
If we cared for any meadow sit were merely
To droop on them and sleep
Our Knees are trembling sorely in the Stooping
We fall upon our faces as we go
And underneath our heavy eyelids drooping
The fairest flowers whould seem as pale as Snow

For all day long we our burden bearing
Through the coal dark underground
Or all day long we drive the wheels of Iron
In the factories round and round
Still all the day the Iron wheels go round
Grinding life down from its mark
And the childrens Souls that God is Calling Sunward
Spin on blindly in the dark

How long ! How long ! Oh cruel nation –
Will you stand to move the world upon a Childs heart
Stifle down with nailed heel its palpitation
And tread onward to the throne amid the mart
Our Blood splashes upward · O gold heaper
And our purple shews your path
And the child sob in the silence curses deeper
Than the strong man in his wrath –

Mrs. Browning's Poem (see page 28) scanned from Charles Lawton's original manuscript.

Stand up Erect! Thou art the form.
and likeness of thy God. A soul as
dauntless mid the storms of daily life.
A heart as pure as breast e'er bore.
What then! Thou art as true a man
as moves
as moves the human mass among,
A much a part of the great plan
with which creations dawn began, as
any in the throng.   Who is thine enemy?
The High in station — or in Wealth thy cheif?
The great — Who cooly pass thee by with
proud steps - and averted eye.   NAY.
nurse not such beleif,
     If true unto thyself thou wast! What
were the proud ones scorn to thee.
A Feather! which thou mightest cast
aside — as idley as the blast. The light
the light leaf from the tree.   NO
Uncurbed passion. low desire - ~~Truth~~ absence
of of Noble Self respect — Death in the breasts
consuming fires to that high nature that
aspires for ever. til thus checked these are
thine enemies — Thy worst. these chain
thee to thy lowly lot — thy labour and thy
life accursed,   O Stand Erect! and from
them burst and longer suffer not —
     Thou art thyself thine enemy. The great
what are they better as theirs - is not thy
will as free? Has God with equal favours thee
neglected to endow. — True - Wealth thou art
not Tis but dust. nor place. uncertain as the
wind — Thou has that with thy daily crust
and water. Mayest despise the lust of both,
A noble mind! and passions under law. True
faith and trust in God, Thou art the peer
of any man! Look up then! that thy
little span of life be nobly trod,

Exhortation (see page 67) scanned from Charles Lawton's original manuscript.

GLOSSARY

After damp	The mixture of gases, present in a mine after an explosion, mainly carbon monoxide.
Bailiff	An agent or land steward.
Banksman	The person in charge of the shaft and cages at the surface of the colliery; the person at the surface who operates the signals to the winding engine and the pit bottom
Black damp	A gas, mainly carbon dioxide, that puts out lamps; also known as chokedamp or stythe
Blower	Gas under pressure escaping from the floor or the walls
Bottomer	Man who cleared the loose coal from the collier's stall, loaded it in the tubs and hauled it to the upshaft, often using the 'bite' harness in places where there was no access for horses.
Brattice	A partition for controlling ventilation. Brattice cloth – a stiffened tarred cloth used for partitions or doors.
Butty	A mate or a partner in a sub-contract
Butty man	A man in charge of others. He was paid for the whole job and paid those under him. A contractor.
Carry water	Drainage water
Corf, corves	A coal miner's basket; now usually a tub or trolley.
Crut	A cross cutting. A road connecting two other more important roads
Dip	Downhill incline of the coal seam
Gin	Old form of winding gear usually powered by horses
Goaf	Waste after the coal has been extracted. Gob, waste often the seat of a fire.
Gutter	Underground drainage tunnel leading from the lowest point of the workings to an adjoining valley. Also known as sough, adit or level or drain. Predating the Newcomen atmospheric steam pumping engine.

GLOSSARY

Heading	A new exploring road into solid strata or a development road in a seam
Hopper	A bucket or kibble, used before cages. Usually called a chair
Kidscrew	Local name for Kidsgrove
Level	A horizontal mine gallery
Marrow	A collier's or hewer's helper. His mate
Migins, midgins	Small flies, midges
Overman	A mine official ranking between Deputy and Under-manager.
Stents	Shifts
Stall	A working place at the coal face.
Thurling	Sometimes thirling. A connecting road, slit, crosscut.
Transports	Convicts shipped off to Australia.
Underviewer	Originally a mining engineer who oversaw several collieries. Head Viewer was a more senior position.
Win, Win peg	Capstan head, capstan bar – turned by horses or men